hamlyn cookery club

Indian flavours

hamlyn cookery club

Indian

flavours

First published in 1999 by Hamlyn
an imprint of Octopus Publishing Group Ltd
2–4 Heron Quays
London E14 4JP

British Library Cataloguing-in-Publication Data
A catalogue record for this book is available from the British Library.

ISBN 0 600 59918 3

Printed in China

Publishing Director: Laura Bamford
Copy Editor: Anne Crane
Creative Director: Keith Martin
Design Manager: Bryan Dunn
Designer: Ginny Zeal
Jacket Photography: Sean Myers
Picture Researcher: Christine Junemann
Senior Production Controller: Katherine Hockley

Notes

1 Both metric and imperial measurements have been given in all recipes. Use one set of measurements only and not a mixture of both.

2 Standard level spoon measurements are used in all recipes.
1 tablespoon = one 15 ml spoon
1 teaspoon = one 5 ml spoon

3 Eggs should be medium unless otherwise stated.

4 Milk should be full fat unless otherwise stated.

5 Fresh herbs should be used unless otherwise stated. If unavailable use dried herbs as an alternative but halve the quantities stated.

6 Pepper should be freshly ground black pepper unless otherwise stated.

7 Ovens should be preheated to the specified temperature – if using a fan-assisted oven, follow the manufacturer's instructions for adjusting the time and temperature.

8 Measurements for canned food have been given as a standard metric equivalent.

Contents

Introduction

The sheer size of the sub-continent, with its vast range of geography and climate, from the snow-capped mountains of the north to the tropical south, means a huge variety of foods, and an enormous variety of ways of cooking them. Among the rich diversity are the tandoori style of cooking which originated in Kashmir, on the north-west frontier, and kebabs from the Middle East. Almonds, peaches, pistachios and fruit-based sherbets, biryanis and pulaos came from Persia, subtly transformed by the conquering Mughals. Coconuts, tamarind and curry leaves are hallmarks of the south, where the food is spicier, while the Portuguese influence is strongly evident in Goa, home of the powerful vindaloo. Religion, too, has played a major part in India's choice of food. The Hindus do not eat beef and the Moslems are forbidden pork, leaving lamb and chicken as the most popular meats, while many people are vegetarian through the dictates of their religion.

Fish and shellfish are popular all around the coast and freshwater fish inland. Vegetables and pulses are an essential part of the Indian diet. Vegetable curries are either cooked dry, the juices from the vegetables supplying the moisture, or with very little sauce. Pulses are made into daals, nourishing purées served with bread and rice. Most Indian breads are unleavened. They are subtly different but interchangeable at the table, so choose according to your taste. Rice dishes range from simple accompaniments such as plain boiled or fried rice, to the festive biryanis, one of the glories of northern Indian cooking. No meal is complete without a raita or chutney. A raita is a refreshing yogurt-based salad, the ideal foil for hot spicy food. Chutneys may be sweet or sour, mild or hot. They may be cooked and left to mature, like an English preserve, or lightly cooked and served at once. Indian desserts are usually milk-based and very rich, so serve in small portions.

Preparing Food Indian-style

Cut all vegetables to the same size and, when making curries, chop the meat into bite-sized pieces. Spices are often dry-roasted for a few seconds to heighten their flavour before they are added to a dish. When cooking an Indian meal, serve a combination of dry curries and moister dishes, and prepare all your ingredients beforehand. Dry-cooked dishes have a way of sticking to the pan and burning if you do not keep an eye on them. No special equipment is needed for Indian cooking. If you have a food processor or a pestle and mortar for making spice pastes and purées and a selection of heavy-based saucepans, you have all you need.

Special Ingredients

A few of the more unusual ingredients used in this book are listed below. Although Indian ingredients are increasingly easy to find in large supermarkets, some of these may be available only from Asian shops.

Baisen flour

A fine yellow flour made from chickpeas and used in breads and batters.

Curry leaves

The green leaves of a tree found in India and Sri Lanka. Found fresh and dry, they are used purely as a flavouring and removed before serving.

Ghee

Also known as clarified butter, this can be heated to a higher temperature than most oils without burning. There are two types of ghee: pure (a dairy product) and vegetable. To make ghee at home melt 250 g (8 oz) unsalted butter in a heavy based pan and simmer for 10–12 minutes. Once the milky white froth has turned golden, strain through muslin and store in a jar.

Kewra water

A very flowery flavouring made from the screwpine plant.

Mango powder

Made from unripe green mangoes, this powder is a useful souring agent.

Snacks

Nimki

Seasoned Flour Crisps

Nimki, or *namak pare*, are diamond-shaped snacks, which can be flavoured with various essences, vegetables or fruits. *Nimkis* can be stored in sealed jars for 1–2 months. When glazed with sugar caramel they become a sweet snack, called *shakar para* or *gauja*.

250 g (8 oz) plain flour
1 teaspoon salt
1 teaspoon caster sugar
1 teaspoon onion seeds
15 g (½ oz) ghee or butter
1 ripe banana, mashed
water, to mix
oil, for deep-frying

Sift the flour, salt and sugar into a bowl, and add the onion seeds. Rub in the ghee or butter, add the banana and enough water to make a soft, smooth dough. Roll out very thinly to about 3 mm (1/8 inch) thickness. Then cut the dough diagonally into strips both ways to make small diamond shapes, and prick with a fork.

Heat the oil in a pan and fry the shapes until golden brown and crisp. Drain the shapes on kitchen paper and allow to cool.

Serves 4

Variations: To make savoury nimki add either freshly ground black pepper or chilli powder to taste, and omit the banana and sugar.

To make *shakar para*, or *gauja*, to serve as a sweet snack, reduce the salt to a pinch and proceed as for the main recipe, with or without the banana filling. Make a rich sugar syrup with 300 g (10 oz) sugar and 500 ml (17 fl oz) water. Dissolve the sugar in the water in a large saucepan, increase the heat and boil until a drop of the syrup forms a hard ball when dropped into a cup of cold water, but before the syrup turns golden. Add the fried *nimki* to the pan and stir to coat with the sugar caramel. *Nimki* are delicious served hot or cold.

Aloo Bonda

Spiced Potato in Batter

Aloo bonda, or *batata wada*, are deep-fried fritters which are a speciality of southern India and Gujurat in the north. This is a very popular dish for all occasions.

140 g (4½ oz) baisen flour
salt
pinch of baking powder
about ½ teaspoon chilli powder
about 150 ml (¼ pint) water

Filling:
500 g (1 lb) potatoes, boiled, peeled and cubed
2 green chillies, deseeded and very finely chopped (optional)
15 g (½ oz) piece of fresh root ginger, peeled and chopped
1 small onion, finely chopped
2 coriander sprigs, chopped
1 tablespoon lemon juice
salt and pepper
oil, for deep-frying

Sift the baisen flour, salt and baking powder into a bowl. Add the chilli powder and sufficient water to make a smooth batter. Beat well, then set aside.

To make the filling, mix together the potatoes, green chillies, ginger, onion, coriander leaves, salt and pepper. Stir in the lemon juice and mix thoroughly. Dip your hands in cold water, then divide the filling into about 20 small balls. Dip these in the batter.

Heat the oil in a pan until a drop of the batter rises quickly and turns crisp. Deep-fry the balls a few at a time until golden brown. Serve hot or cold with tomato ketchup or a chutney.

Serves 4

Variation: Instead of the lemon juice use 3 teaspoons mango powder or 1 tablespoon tamarind liquid.

Samosas

Meat-stuffed Pastries

150 g (5 oz) plain flour
pinch of salt
¼ teaspoon baking powder
25 g (1 oz) ghee or butter
water, to mix
oil, for deep-frying
Filling:
15 g (½ oz) ghee or 1 tablespoon oil
1 onion, chopped
250 g (8 oz) lean minced beef
1 green chilli, deseeded and very finely chopped
2–3 coriander sprigs, chopped
juice of ½ lemon or 2 teaspoons mango powder
salt and pepper
Flour paste:
2–3 teaspoons plain flour mixed with a little water

Sift the flour, salt and baking powder into a bowl, and rub in the ghee or butter. Add enough water to make a soft smooth dough. Cover and set aside.

To make the filling, heat the ghee or oil in a saucepan and lightly fry the onion. Add the mince and salt and pepper. Add a little water and gently fry the mince for 10–12 minutes until dry, stirring occasionally. Add the green chilli, coriander and lemon juice or mango powder and mix well. Remove from the heat and allow to cool.

Meanwhile, knead the dough well and divide into 16–18 even-sized balls. Using a little flour, roll out one portion into a 10–12 cm (4–5 inch) round. Cut across the centre, then apply the flour paste down the straight edge and bring the two corners together to make a cone, gently pressing the pasted edges together to secure.

Fill the cone with the filling, apply flour paste to the open mouth of the cone and seal the shape. Prepare the remaining samosas in the same way.

Heat the oil in a deep frying pan and gently deep-fry the samosas, a few at a time, until golden brown. Drain on kitchen paper and serve hot or cold with tomato ketchup or a chutney.

Makes 16–18

Variations: To make vegetable samosas substitute the following for lean mince: 500 g (1 lb) potatoes, boiled, peeled and cubed or 500 g (1 lb) mixed peas, diced carrots, green beans and potatoes. Add 1 teaspoon garam masala to the spices.

***above:** nimki, aloo bonda, samosas*

Kabuli Channa

Chickpea Snack

250 g (8 oz) chickpeas
1 teaspoon bicarbonate of soda
40 g (1½ oz) block tamarind
2 teaspoons brown sugar
250 g (8 oz) potatoes, boiled, peeled and quartered
2 coriander sprigs, chopped
1–2 green chillies, deseeded and very finely chopped
1 onion, chopped
15 g (½ oz) cumin seeds, dry-roasted and ground
juice of 1 lemon (optional)
salt and pepper

Wash the chickpeas in cold water and soak them overnight with the bicarbonate of soda added to the soaking water.

Drain the chickpeas and put them in a saucepan, adding enough fresh water to cover and cook until soft in the centre. Allow to cool, then remove the lid and boil rapidly to evaporate the excess liquid.

Break up the tamarind and soak in 175 ml (6 fl oz) boiling water for 10–15 minutes then press through a sieve to extract as much liquid as possible. Discard the pulp. Stir the brown sugar thoroughly into the tamarind liquid and set aside. Mix together the chickpeas, potatoes, coriander, chillies, onion and salt and pepper. Pour the tamarind mixture

on top and stir well. Scatter over the ground cumin seeds, sprinkle with lemon juice and serve.

Serves 4

Variations: To make a spicier version, sprinkle the dish with garam masala and chilli powder.

Chopped or sliced fruit and vegetables can be mixed in with the other ingredients; this dish is called a *chaat*. The following are all suitable: bananas, pears, apples, pineapples, peaches, papayas, mangoes, guavas, cucumbers, tomatoes and radishes.

Halim

Spiced Beef or Lamb with Wheat

Halim can be served at any meal and can be stored in the freezer as this does not affect its flavour.

If wheat in whole or broken form is not readily available from Asian stores or health food shops, a mixture of oats, barley and split chickpeas (*channa daal*) in any proportion will give a good result.

Garam masala or chilli powder can be sprinkled on the finished dish to make it more spicy.

***left:** kabuli channa, halim*

250 g (8 oz) whole or broken wheat
salt
Spicy Meat Sauce:
25 g (1 oz) ghee or butter
250 g (8 oz) onions, chopped
2–3 x 2.5 cm (1 inch) cinnamon sticks
8–10 cloves
8–10 small green cardamoms
4 large cardamoms
1–2 bay leaves
1 kg (2 lb) lean beef or lamb, diced
50 g (2 oz) piece of fresh root ginger, ground to a paste
7–8 garlic cloves, crushed
2½ teaspoons ground cumin
about 1 teaspoon chilli powder
1 teaspoon ground turmeric
150 g (5 oz) natural yogurt
1.2 litres (2 pints) water
To serve:
125 g (4 oz) butter, melted
pepper
25 g (1 oz) piece of fresh ginger root, peeled and finely chopped
2 green chillies, deseeded and very finely chopped
3–4 coriander sprigs, chopped
2 lemons, cut into wedges
500 g (1 lb) onions, sliced and crisply fried

Wash the wheat thoroughly in cold water and dry on kitchen paper. If using whole wheat crush it coarsely using a tea towel and a rolling pin. Leave the wheat to soak overnight in cold water.

Drain the wheat then place it in a saucepan with water to cover and a pinch of salt. Cook the wheat for 40–55 minutes until it is soft, and has the consistency of porridge, stirring occasionally to prevent sticking. Alternatively use a pressure cooker and cook for about 15 minutes. When cooked, drain and set aside.

To make the sauce, heat the ghee or butter in a large, preferably nonstick, saucepan and fry the chopped onions until golden brown. Add the cinnamon sticks, cloves, cardamoms and bay leaves and continue frying for 15–20 seconds. Add the meat, ginger, garlic, cumin, chilli powder, turmeric and yogurt. Mix well and cover with a lid. Cook gently for about 20–30 minutes until the mixture is nearly dry.

Increase the heat and fry the mixture for 1–2 minutes, then add the water. Cover and simmer for about 20 minutes until the meat is tender.

Add the cooked wheat to the mixture, cover and cook for 40–50 minutes over a very gentle heat, stirring frequently. Add a little extra water if the mixture is becoming too thick.

Serve piping hot with the melted butter poured over and pepper to taste. Garnish with chopped ginger, chilli, coriander leaves, lemon wedge and fried onion.

Serves 4

Pakoras

Pakoras are deep-fried fruit or vegetable fritters. The batter is made with a special flour, called *baisen*, which is the flour of the *channa* (chickpea), or Bengal gram as it is sometimes known.

125 g (4 oz) potato, cut into ⅛ inch slices
125 g (4 oz) onion, sliced into rings
125 g (4 oz) cauliflower florets
125 g (4 oz) aubergine, sliced
125 g (4 oz) green pepper, cored, deseeded and sliced into rings
Batter:
140 g (4½ oz) baisen flour
pinch of baking powder
about ½ teaspoon chilli powder
salt
about 75 ml (3 fl oz) water
juice of ½ lemon
oil, for deep-frying

To make the batter, sift the baisen flour, baking powder, chilli powder and salt into a bowl. Add the water to make a smooth batter. Add the lemon juice and beat well. Set aside.

Heat the oil in a pan until a drop of batter in the oil rises quickly and turns crisp. Dip the vegetable pieces into the batter a few at a time and deep-fry them until golden brown and crisp. Drain on kitchen paper and keep hot while deep-frying the rest. Serve hot with tomato ketchup or a chutney.

Serves 4

Variations: Other sliced fruits and vegetables you can use instead are semi-ripe bananas, pineapples, apples, mushrooms, firm tomatoes, or thickly shredded cabbage or spinach. You can also try cubes of chicken or fish. To make shapes of batter without any filling, make a much thicker batter and add 1 teaspoon cumin seeds.

Tali Hui Jhninga

Spiced Fried Prawns

500 g (1 lb) large cooked prawns
2 tablespoons tamarind water
pinch of ground turmeric
1 teaspoon grated fresh root ginger
2 shallots or ½ onion, sliced
2 garlic cloves, crushed
1 tablespoon light soy sauce
150 ml (¼ pint) oil
Batter:
75 g (3 oz) rice flour or plain flour
4 tablespoons water
1 small egg, beaten
salt and pepper

Discard the heads and shells from the prawns, but leave on the tails. Devein them. Place the prawns in a bowl with the tamarind water, turmeric, ginger, shallots, garlic and soy sauce. Stir well and leave to marinate for 30 minutes.

Meanwhile, make the batter. Place the flour in a bowl and gradually add the water. Add salt and pepper to taste, then gradually beat in the egg.

Drain the marinade from the prawns and shallots. Dip the prawns and shallots in the batter. Heat the oil in a frying pan or wok and add the prawns and shallots, one at a time, until the bottom is covered. Fry until golden brown and crisp, then turn over and fry the underside. Serve hot or cold.

Serves 4

Note: This dish should really be made with freshly cooked prawns, but it is still delicious with ready-cooked prawns from the fishmonger. Serve it with basmati rice.

Dosas

Pancakes

250 g (8 oz) urhad daal (dried pulses or lentils)
50 g (2 oz) long-grain rice
600 ml (1 pint) water
½ teaspoon bicarbonate of soda
1 teaspoon chilli powder
½ teaspoon salt
vegetable oil, for shallow-frying

Wash the daal and rice thoroughly, then put them into a bowl with the water and leave to soak overnight.

Place the daal, rice and water mixture in a blender or food processor and work until smooth. Add the bicarbonate of soda, chilli powder and salt and stir well.

Pour in enough batter to cover the bottom of a cold heavy-based pan. Put on the heat until the batter starts to set. Pour about 1 teaspoon oil around the edge of the dosa, then shake the pan to spread the oil. Fry the pancake for about 1 minute, until golden underneath. Remove the pancake from the pan and roll it up, enclosing a filling if liked. Repeat with the remaining batter. Serve hot.

Makes 12–15

Note: You can serve *dosas* as plain pancakes, or filled with a stuffing. Try filling them with a spiced and flavoured rice such as Prawn and Spinach Rice (see page 67).

Steamed Lentil Cakes

375 g (12 oz) red lentils
1.8 litres (3 pints) cold water
1 teaspoon ground cumin
1 teaspoon chilli powder
1 teaspoon salt
½ teaspoon black peppercorns, crushed
25 g (1 oz) coriander leaves, chopped
juice of 1 lemon
250 g (8 oz) natural yogurt

Wash the lentils. Drain, place in a bowl and add the cold water. Leave to soak overnight.

Drain the water and grind the lentils to a fine paste in a food processor. Using muslin or a tea towel, squeeze the excess water from the lentils.

Transfer the lentil paste to a bowl and add the cumin, chilli powder, salt, pepper and coriander leaves. Shape into 6–8 cakes, 5 cm (2 inches) in diameter and 1 cm (½ inch) thick. Pat them dry with absorbent kitchen paper.

Place the lentil cakes in the top of a steamer, cover and steam for 1 hour. Alternatively, place the lentil cakes in a shallow dish, stand it in a roasting tin filled with enough hot water to come halfway up the sides of the dish. Cover the dish and tin with foil, then bake in a preheated oven, 190°C (375°F), Gas Mark 5, for 1 hour. Remove the foil and leave to cool.

Mix the lemon juice with the yogurt. Place the lentil cakes in a shallow dish and cover with the yogurt mixture. Refrigerate for at least 2 hours before serving.

Makes 6–8

Ekuri

Spicy Scrambled Eggs

50 g (2 oz) butter
1 onion, finely chopped
2 green chillies, finely chopped
8 eggs, lightly beaten with 2 tablespoons water
1 tablespoon finely chopped coriander leaves
salt

Heat the butter in a pan, add the onion and fry until deep golden. Add the chillies and fry for 30 seconds, then add the beaten eggs, coriander leaves and salt to taste. Cook, stirring constantly, until the eggs are lightly scrambled and set. Serve hot.

Serves 4

Note: Hot, fresh green chillies should be used for this recipe, but use with care. For a less pungent result slit the chillies, discard the seeds and rinse under a tap. Chillies are included in many of the recipes in this book and are used in amounts which ensure an authentic Indian taste. Quantities can be adjusted to suit personal taste: if you are unfamiliar with chillies, you may wish to start with relatively modest amounts, building up the heat as you become more used to them.
Handle chillies with care, wear gloves if your hands are sensitive, and be careful not to touch any part of your face, particularly your eyes, before you have washed your hands.

above: *ekuri*
left: *steamed lentil cakes*

Fish and Shellfish

Prawns with Tamarind

25 g (1 oz) block tamarind
1 small red pepper, cored, deseeded and chopped
25 g (1 oz) small onions, chopped
2 garlic cloves, chopped
1 red chilli, deseeded and chopped
1 tablespoon ground lemon grass
6 tablespoons oil
4 teaspoons caster sugar
2 teaspoons lime juice
500 g (1 lb) unpeeled Mediterranean prawns, heads left on and deveined through the shell
salt
watercress, to serve

Break up the tamarind and soak in 175 ml (6 fl oz) boiling water for 10–15 minutes then press through a sieve to extract as much liquid as possible. Discard the pulp.

Place the red pepper, onions, garlic, chilli and lemon grass in a liquidizer or food processor and blend. Heat the oil in a pan, add the pepper mixture and stir-fry for 5 minutes. Gradually blend in the tamarind liquid, sugar, lime juice and salt to taste. Add the prawns and stir-fry for 5 minutes or until the prawns are just firm to the touch. Serve with watercress.

Serves 4

Curried Crab

1 fresh coconut
600 ml (1 pint) boiling water
75 g (3 oz) ghee
1 large onion, sliced
4 garlic cloves, sliced
7.5 cm (3 inch) piece of fresh root ginger, peeled and thinly sliced
2 teaspoons fenugreek seeds
2 teaspoons peppercorns
2 teaspoons chilli powder
2 teaspoons ground coriander
1 teaspoon ground turmeric
1 teaspoon salt
500 g (1 lb) natural yogurt
300 ml (½ pint) milk
500 g (1 lb) crab meat

To prepare the coconut milk, make holes in the eyes of the coconut, pour out the liquid and reserve. Crack open the coconut and cut out the flesh. Thinly slice quarter of the flesh and blend the remainder in a liquidizer. Add the water, stir for 5 minutes then strain through a piece of muslin. Mix the coconut juice with the prepared coconut milk.

Heat the ghee in a pan, add the onion, garlic and ginger and fry for 5 minutes. Add the spices and salt. Stir and fry for 2–3 minutes, then add the coconut milk. Mix the yogurt with the milk and stir into the pan. Bring to just below boiling point and simmer for 5–6 minutes.

Add the crab meat and sliced coconut and cook gently for 5 minutes. Serve at once.

Serves 6

left: *prawns with tamarind*
above: *bhoona prawns*

Bhoona Prawns

Dry Prawn Curry

2 tablespoons oil
1 onion, diced
500 g (1 lb) peeled prawns
3 garlic cloves, crushed
1½ teaspoons garam masala
about 1½ teaspoons chilli powder
½ teaspoon ground turmeric
200 ml (7 fl oz) water
salt

To garnish:
1–2 green chillies, deseeded and very finely chopped
2–3 coriander sprigs, chopped
lemon juice
1–2 tomatoes, sliced (optional)

Heat the oil in a pan and gently fry the onion until tender. Add the prawns and continue frying until dry. Add the garlic, garam masala, chilli powder and turmeric, stir well and fry for 30 seconds. Add salt to taste and the water. Cover and cook gently for 10–15 minutes until dry.

Garnish with the chopped chilli and coriander, sprinkle with lemon juice to taste and arrange the tomato slices on top, if liked. Serve as a side dish with rice and bread.

Serves 4

Fish Molee

750 g (1½ lb) cod fillet, skinned and cut into 4 pieces
2 tablespoons plain flour
4 tablespoons oil
2 onions, sliced
2 garlic cloves, crushed
1 teaspoon ground turmeric
4 green chillies, finely chopped
2 tablespoons lemon juice
175 ml (6 fl oz) coconut milk
salt
fresh herbs, to garnish

Coat the fish with the flour. Heat the oil in a frying pan, add the fish, and fry quickly on both sides. Remove and set aside.

Add the onion and garlic and fry until soft and golden. Add the turmeric, chillies, lemon juice, coconut milk and salt to taste. Simmer, uncovered, for 10 minutes until thickened. Return the fish, spoon over the sauce and cook for 2–3 minutes. Garnish and serve.

Serves 4

Goan Mussels

1 kg (2 lb) mussels
125 g (4 oz) ghee or butter
1 large onion, chopped
2 garlic cloves, chopped
2 teaspoons desiccated coconut
2 teaspoons salt
1 teaspoon ground turmeric
1 teaspoon chilli powder
1 teaspoon pepper
150 ml (¼ pint) vinegar
500 g (1 lb) natural yogurt
2 teaspoons garam masala
juice of 2 lemons

To prepare the mussels, scrub them with a stiff brush, then use a small sharp knife to scrape off the beards and any barnacles. Wash thoroughly in cold water and discard any open mussels.

Heat the ghee or butter in a large saucepan, add the onion and garlic and fry for 5 minutes. Add the coconut and salt and fry until browned. Add the turmeric, chilli powder and pepper and fry for 1 minute. Add the vinegar and mussels, cover the pan and bring to the boil. Cook for about 5 minutes or until the shells open, then remove the pan from the heat.

Remove the empty shells and discard. Arrange the remaining mussels in a warmed serving dish. Pour the cooking liquid into a liquidizer or food processor with the yogurt and garam masala and blend for 1 minute. Reheat until hot but not boiling. Pour the sauce over the mussels, sprinkle with lemon juice and serve at once.

Serves 4

***above:** fish molee*
***right:** tali machli*

Tandoori Sole

300 g (10 oz) natural yogurt
2 garlic cloves, crushed
2 drops red food colouring
½ teaspoon chilli powder
½ teaspoon ground turmeric
½ teaspoon ground coriander
½ teaspoon ground cumin
1 teaspoon ground ginger
½ teaspoon garam masala
salt and pepper
2 lemon sole, skinned and filleted
To garnish:
lime or lemon wedges
coriander sprigs

Put the yogurt, garlic and red food colouring into a shallow bowl and mix together. Add the chilli powder, turmeric, coriander, cumin, ginger and garam masala with salt and pepper to taste and stir well. Add the fish and spoon over the tandoori mixture then cover and leave to marinate for 1 hour.

Pour boiling water into a roasting tin to come halfway up the sides. Put a grill rack in the tin and place the marinated fish on the rack. Pour any remaining marinade over the fish. Cook in a preheated oven, 180°C (350°F), Gas Mark 4, for 15 minutes. Serve at once garnished with lime or lemon wedges and coriander sprigs.

Serves 2

Tali Machli

Dry Spiced Fish

Instead of frying the fish it can be arranged in a baking dish, brushed with oil and placed under a preheated grill or baked in a preheated oven, 180°C (350°F), Gas Mark 4, for 15–20 minutes.

about 1 teaspoon chilli powder
1 teaspoon ground cumin
1 teaspoon mango powder or
 2 teaspoons lemon juice
4 x 175 g (6 oz) white fish fillets,
 rinsed and dried
3 coriander sprigs, ground to a paste
1 garlic clove, crushed
1 green chilli, deseeded and crushed
 (optional)
1 teaspoon garam masala
lemon juice (optional)
salt and pepper
oil, for frying
To garnish:
lime wedges
coriander sprigs

Mix together the chilli powder, cumin, mango powder or lemon juice and salt and pepper. Sprinkle over the fish fillets.

Combine the coriander, garlic and the crushed chilli. Rub this mixture well into the fish and sprinkle with garam masala. It may be necessary to use a little lemon juice to help the mixture adhere. Set aside for 7–10 minutes.

Heat a little oil in a frying pan and fry the fish fillets, two at a time, for about 5 minutes on each side. Keep warm while frying the remainder. Serve hot, garnished with lime wedges and coriander.

Serves 4

Tomatar Jhinga

Prawn Curry with Tomato

2–3 tablespoon oil
2 onions, cut into cubes
2.5 cm (1 inch) cinnamon stick
2 bay leaves
500 g (1 lb) peeled raw prawns, rinsed and drained
5–6 garlic cloves, crushed
25 g (1 oz) piece of fresh root ginger, crushed, or 1 teaspoon ground ginger
about 1 teaspoon chilli powder
1½ teaspoons ground cumin
1 teaspoon ground coriander
225 g (7½ oz) can tomatoes
1 teaspoon garam masala
125 g (4 oz) green pepper, cored, deseeded and finely chopped
salt
To garnish:
1–2 green chillies, seeded and very finely chopped
1–2 coriander sprigs, chopped

Heat the oil in a large saucepan and fry the onions until just tender. Add the cinnamon and the bay leaves, fry for 15 seconds, then add the prawns. Stir over the heat for 30 seconds.

Stir in the garlic, ginger, chilli, cumin and the coriander. Fry for 30 seconds, add the tomatoes and garam masala, and mix well. Add salt to taste, cover and simmer gently for at least 15 minutes, until the prawns are cooked. Stir in a little water if necessary then add the green pepper a few minutes before removing from the heat.

Garnish with the chopped chillies and coriander leaves. Serve as a main dish with rice or bread.

Serves 4

Prawn Sukke

Prawn Curry with Coconut

This curry comes from the Malabar coast of India and has a distinctly southern flavour, using coconut and tamarind in its ingredients.

25 g (1 oz) block tamarind
500 g (1 lb) peeled raw prawns
50 g (2 oz) desiccated coconut
500 ml (17 fl oz) water
25 g (1 oz) creamed coconut
125 g (4 oz) frozen peas
4–5 curry leaves
1 green chilli, deseeded and cut in half
40 g (1½ oz) piece of fresh root ginger, peeled and finely chopped
2 tomatoes, skinned and diced
25 g (1 oz) ghee or 2 tablespoons oil
1 teaspoon fenugreek seeds
2 teaspoons ground coriander or coriander seeds
2 small whole red chillies (optional)
1 large onion, chopped
salt

Break up the tamarind and soak in 175 ml (6 fl oz) boiling water for 10–15 minutes then press through a sieve to extract as much liquid as possible. Discard the pulp.

Meanwhile, rinse the prawns and drain them well. Put the desiccated coconut into a bowl with 300 ml (½ pint) of the water and leave for 10 minutes.

Blend the desiccated coconut with its soaking liquid and strain to get a creamy milk. Reserve the leftover pulp. Put the creamy milk in a pan, add the creamed coconut, peas, curry leaves, green chilli, ginger, tomatoes and tamarind water, cover and leave to simmer.

Heat 1 teaspoon of the ghee or oil in a separate pan and gently fry the fenugreek seeds, coriander and red chillies until the fenugreek turns light brown. Do not let the mixture burn. Remove the pan from the heat, leave to cool, then blend this mixture with the reserved coconut pulp and the remaining water to make a fine paste.

Heat a further 1 tablespoon of the ghee or oil and fry the prawns until dry. Add the blended paste and gently fry for 5–6 minutes. Then stir into the simmering coconut milk mixture and season with salt to taste. Simmer the paste, covered, for 15–20 minutes.

To serve, fry the onion in the remaining ghee or oil then spoon it over the prawn curry. Serve with boiled rice.

Serves 4

Machli Ka Salan

Fish Curry

If you use frozen fish, which flakes easily, it is a good idea to add the fish towards the end of the cooking. Alternatively, the fish can be fried separately and added to the sauce, or the dish can be cooked in a preheated oven, 160°C (325°F), Gas Mark 3, for about 40 minutes. Cod, hake, halibut, coley, haddock, plaice or whiting are all suitable for this recipe.

above: *prawn sukke, tomatar jhinga, machli ka salan*

40 g (1½ oz) ghee or 3 tablespoons oil
2 onions, chopped
25 g (1 oz) piece of fresh root ginger, peeled and crushed
4–5 garlic cloves, crushed
½ teaspoon ground turmeric
about 1 teaspoon chilli powder
1 teaspoon ground cumin
1 teaspoon ground coriander
1 teaspoon garam masala
500 g (1 lb) white fish fillets, cut into 2.5 cm (1 inch) pieces
400 g (13 oz) can tomatoes
1 teaspoon salt
1 green chilli, halved and deseeded
To garnish:
1 green pepper, cored, deseeded and finely chopped (optional)
chopped coriander leaves (optional)

Heat the ghee or oil in a large saucepan and fry the onions until light brown. Add the ginger, garlic, turmeric, chilli powder, cumin, coriander and garam masala. Fry for 15 seconds, then add the fish pieces and stir gently.

Add the tomatoes, salt and chilli. Cover and cook gently for 5–10 minutes or until the fish is tender. Remove from the heat and add the chopped green pepper and chopped coriander leaves, if liked. If preferred remove the chilli halves, then serve with bread or rice.

Serves 4

Madras Mackerel Curry

Madras is the main city of southern India and because of its close proximity to the sea fish dishes are very popular. Southern Indian food tends to be more spicy than that in the north. This recipe uses unfilleted mackerel but for a less authentic version filleted fish may be substituted.

25 g (1 oz) block tamarind
2 tablespoons oil
1 onion, crushed or finely chopped
3 garlic cloves, crushed
about 1 teaspoon chilli powder
¼ teaspoon ground turmeric
1½ teaspoons ground coriander
½ teaspoon cumin seeds, dry roasted and ground
½ teaspoon mustard seeds, dry roasted and ground
½ teaspoon fenugreek seeds, dry roasted and ground
½ teaspoon desiccated coconut
4–5 curry leaves
225 g (7½ oz) can tomatoes
500 g (1 lb) mackerel, cleaned and cut into 5 cm (2 inch) pieces
1 green chilli, deseeded and very finely chopped
salt
To garnish:
25 g (1 oz) ghee or 2 tablespoons oil
1 onion, chopped
1 teaspoon cumin seeds
coriander leaves
piece of red chilli

Break up the tamarind and soak in 125 ml (4 fl oz) boiling water for 10–15 minutes then press through a sieve to extract as much liquid as possible. Discard the pulp.

Heat the oil in a large saucepan and fry the onion until light brown. Add the garlic, chilli powder, turmeric, coriander, cumin, mustard seeds, fenugreek, coconut and curry leaves. Fry gently for 30 seconds. Add the tamarind liquid and the tomatoes to the spices and simmer gently for 1 minute.

Carefully add the mackerel, then the chopped chilli and salt. Cover and cook for 30–40 minutes. If necessary add a little water.

To garnish, heat the ghee or oil and fry the chopped onion until light brown. Add the cumin seeds and as soon as they begin to crackle, pour the mixture over the fish curry. Serve garnished with a piece of red chilli and some coriander leaves, and serve at once with plain boiled rice.

Serves 4

Masale Vali Machli

Dry Fried Herring

about 1 teaspoon chilli powder
1½ teaspoons ground turmeric
1 teaspoon ground ginger
1 teaspoon crushed garlic
pinch of salt and pepper
500 g (1 lb) herring fillets, with or without roes, cut into 5 cm (2 inch) pieces
oil, for frying
To garnish:
lemon slices
mint sprigs

Mix together the chilli powder, turmeric, ginger, garlic and salt and pepper. Rub the mixture into the fish pieces and set aside to marinate for 10–15 minutes. Heat a little oil and fry the fish pieces in two batches until golden brown. Remove the fish and drain on kitchen paper. Serve hot, garnished with lemon slices.

Serves 4

above left: *Madras mackerel curry*
above right: *masale vali machli, Goan mackerel curry*

Goan Mackerel Curry

Until the early '60s Goa was a Portuguese territory; the combination of Indian and Portuguese cooking styles has produced many famous dishes such as *vindaloo* and Goan curries, and certain pickles. Unfilleted fish is used in this curry for flavour and appearance, but filleted mackerel may be substituted.

15 g (½ oz) block tamarind
2 tablespoons oil
1 small onion, chopped
about 1 teaspoon chilli powder
½ teaspoon ground cumin
2 teaspoons ground coriander
125 g (4 oz) desiccated coconut
½ teaspoon ground turmeric
225 g (7½ oz) can tomatoes, roughly chopped
5–6 curry leaves
1–2 green chillies, deseeded and very finely chopped
200 ml (7 fl oz) water
500 g (1 lb) mackerel, cleaned and cut into 2.5 cm (1 inch) pieces
salt
To garnish:
lemon or lime wedges
flat leaf parsley sprigs

Break up the tamarind and soak in 75 ml (3 fl oz) boiling water for 10–15 minutes then press through a sieve to extract as much liquid as possible. Discard the pulp.

Heat the oil in a large saucepan and fry the onion until light brown. Add the chilli powder, cumin, coriander, coconut and turmeric. Fry for 30 seconds.

Stir in the tomatoes, tamarind liquid, curry leaves, chilli and salt. Add the water. Carefully stir in the mackerel, cover and simmer gently for 20–30 minutes until the fish is tender. Garnish with lemon or lime wedges and flat leaf parsley sprigs and serve with plain boiled rice.

Serves 4

Fish Tandoori

4 halibut steaks, about 175 g (6 oz) each
50 g (2 oz) natural yogurt
2 tablespoons oil
2 tablespoons paprika
1 tablespoon ground cumin
1 teaspoon ground fennel seeds
1 teaspoon chilli powder
salt
To garnish:
1 small lettuce, shredded
1 fennel bulb, sliced

Wash the fish and pat dry with kitchen paper.

Combine the yogurt, oil, paprika, cumin, fennel and chilli powder in a large bowl with salt to taste and mix well. Place the fish in the bowl and rub well with the tandoori mixture. Cover and leave to marinate for 4–5 hours.

Transfer the marinated fish to a shallow ovenproof baking dish and bake uncovered in a preheated oven, 180°C (350°F), Gas Mark 4, for 20–25 minutes. Arrange the lettuce on a warmed serving dish. Lift the fish on to the lettuce and spoon over the juices. Garnish with the fennel and serve at once.

Serves 4

Vinegar Fish

This is a recipe from the west coast of India. Here sourness is introduced with vinegar instead of in the more usual way with tamarind. Serve with a lentil *daal, roti* and natural yogurt.

1 teaspoon ground turmeric
1 teaspoon salt
500 g (1 lb) haddock or cod steaks
3 tablespoons oil
2 onions, sliced
2–3 green chillies, thinly sliced
2 garlic cloves
2.5 cm (1 inch) piece of fresh root ginger, peeled and cut into strips
2 tablespoons white wine vinegar
4 tablespoons water
coriander sprigs, to garnish

Mix together the turmeric and salt on a plate. Coat the fish in the mixture. Heat the oil in a frying pan, add the fish and fry gently on both sides for 1–2 minutes. Lift out the fish and set aside.

Add the onions, chillies, garlic and ginger and fry, stirring, until golden. Stir in the vinegar and water. Return the fish, cover the pan and cook gently for 5–6 minutes or until cooked through.

To serve, transfer the fish to a warmed serving dish and garnish with the coriander.

Serves 4

above: *vinegar fish*
right: *dahi wali macchi*

Dahi Wali Macchi

Baked Spiced Fish

250 g (8 oz) natural yogurt
1 onion, chopped
1 garlic clove, chopped
1 teaspoon grated fresh root ginger
1 tablespoon vinegar
1½ teaspoons ground cumin
pinch of chilli powder
1 kg (2 lb) whole fish or 750 g (1½ lb) fish fillets (see note)
juice of 1 lemon
1 teaspoon salt

To garnish:
lemon slices
fresh coriander leaves

Put 50 g (2 oz) of the yogurt, the onion, garlic, ginger, vinegar, cumin and chilli powder into a liquidizer or food processor and blend to a smooth paste. Add the remaining yogurt.

Score the fish and place it in an ovenproof dish. Rub with lemon juice and sprinkle with the salt. Pour over the yogurt marinade, cover and leave to marinate overnight.

Cover the fish with foil and bake in a preheated oven, 180°C (350°F), Gas Mark 4, for 30 minutes. Serve hot, garnished with lemon slices and coriander leaves.

Serves 4

Note: When picking fish for this dish you will find that whole fish give the best results – try bream or snapper for example. If using fillets, choose cod or a similar chunky fish, or use fish steaks.

Spinach with Prawns

50 g (2 oz) ghee or 4 tablespoons oil
1 large onion, sliced
2 garlic cloves, sliced
1 tablespoon tomato purée
½ teaspoon garam masala
1½ teaspoons ground coriander
½ teaspoon ground turmeric
½ teaspoon chilli powder
½ teaspoon ground ginger
1 teaspoon salt
500 g (1 lb) frozen whole leaf spinach
500 g (1 lb) cooked peeled prawns

Melt the ghee in a large saucepan, add the onion and garlic and fry gently for 4–5 minutes until soft. Stir in the tomato purée and fry, stirring constantly, for 1 minute. Add the spices and salt and fry for a further 5 minutes, stirring constantly.

Add the frozen spinach and break up with a wooden spoon. Cook until the spinach has thoroughly defrosted, about 3–4 minutes, stirring frequently. Add the prawns and cook for a further 5 minutes, turning gently to coat with the spinach. Serve at once.

Serves 4

Meat

Pork Vindaloo

Although very little pork is eaten in India, this dish is a speciality of Goa. *Vindaloo* dishes always contain vinegar.

120 ml (4 fl oz) vinegar
500 g (1 lb) lean pork, cubed
1 large onion, roughly chopped
1 teaspoon cumin seeds
2 teaspoons mustard seeds
5–6 garlic cloves, crushed
15 g (½ oz) piece of fresh root ginger, peeled
4 cloves
2.5 cm (1 inch) cinnamon stick
6–8 peppercorns
40 g (½ oz) ghee or 3 tablespoons oil
6–8 curry leaves
500 g (1 lb) tomatoes, skinned and chopped
½ teaspoon ground turmeric
salt
chopped coriander, to garnish

Blend 1 tablespoon of the vinegar with a little water and rinse the pork in this mixture. Drain and pat dry with kitchen paper. Put the onion, cumin seeds, mustard seeds, garlic, ginger, cloves, cinnamon and peppercorns into a bowl and work to a thick paste with a little of the remaining vinegar. In a large bowl or dish thoroughly mix the pork cubes with the spice paste. Cover and set aside to marinate for 15–20 minutes.

Heat the ghee or oil in a saucepan and fry the curry leaves until golden brown. Add the marinated pork, tomatoes and turmeric, and keep stirring until the tomatoes are completely broken up. Add the remaining vinegar and salt to taste. Cover and simmer for about 40–50 minutes, until the pork is tender. A little water may be added during cooking if necessary, although the sauce should be fairly thick.

Garnish with coriander and serve with rice, if liked.

Serves 4

Seekh Kebabs

If you do not have many skewers, it may be necessary to make the kebabs in batches and keep them warm.

1 green chilli, deseeded and very finely chopped
15 g (½ oz) piece of fresh root ginger, peeled
3–5 garlic cloves, peeled
1–2 coriander sprigs, finely chopped
1 teaspoon cumin seeds
10 peppercorns
6 cloves
6 small cardamoms
500 g (1 lb) lean minced beef or lamb
1 small onion, very finely chopped
about ½ teaspoon chilli powder
1 small egg, beaten
salt
a little oil, for brushing
lemon slices, to serve (optional)

Grind the green chilli, ginger, garlic, coriander leaves, cumin seeds, peppercorns, cloves and cardamoms to a paste, adding a little water if necessary. Mix together the meat and onion and stir in the spice paste, chilli powder and salt. Add enough beaten egg to make a firm consistency and mix thoroughly. Set the mixture aside for 2–3 minutes to allow the egg to bind it together.

Rub a skewer with a little oil. Shape some of the meat mixture around the skewer to a length of about 10 cm (4 inches). Repeat with the other skewers.

Place the kebabs on a grill pan and cook them under a preheated grill for 2–3 minutes on each side, brushing them with a little oil if necessary when you turn them over. Alternatively, arrange the kebabs on a wire rack on a baking sheet and cook them in a preheated oven, 190°C (375°F), Gas Mark 5, for 15–20 minutes, turning them to cook them evenly. These kebabs are also delicious cooked on a barbecue.

Serve with lemon slices if liked.

Makes about 12

Bholar Gosht

Beef with Green Peppers

50 g (2 oz) butter
500 g (1 lb) braising steak, cut into narrow strips about 5 cm (2 inches) long
1 onion, chopped
50 g (2 oz) raisins
1 large green pepper, cored, deseeded and cut into strips
50 g (2 oz) desiccated coconut
1 teaspoon chilli powder
1 teaspoon garam masala
1 teaspoon ground cinnamon
1 teaspoon salt

Heat the butter in a large frying pan. Add the beef, onion and raisins and stir-fry for about 5 minutes. Cover and cook over a low heat for 30–35 minutes until the meat is tender and there is no liquid left in the pan. Add the green pepper, coconut, chilli powder, garam masala, cinnamon and salt and stir-fry for a further 2–3 minutes. The finished dish should be dry and the green pepper crunchy. Serve with poppadoms and plain boiled rice.

Serves 4

below: *pork vindaloo, seekh kebabs*

Chops Masale Vale

Dry Spiced Lamb Chops

8 chump or loin lamb chops
about ½ teaspoon chilli powder
2 teaspoons ground ginger
1 garlic clove, crushed
150 g (5 oz) natural yogurt
about 1 tablespoon oil
salt and pepper
To garnish:
lemon or lime wedges
fried onion rings
coriander sprigs

Put the chops into a large bowl or dish and sprinkle over the chilli powder, ginger, garlic and salt and pepper. Add the yogurt, mix well, cover and leave them to marinate for 1–2 hours.

Pour the oil on to the marinated chops and mix again thoroughly. Lift the chops out of the marinade and cook them under a preheated hot grill for 4–6 minutes on each side until tender. Serve the chops hot, garnished with lemon or lime wedges, fried onion rings and coriander sprigs.

Serves 4

Variation: Instead of grilling the chops, heat 1 tablespoon of oil in a large pan and fry 1 chopped onion until tender. Add the marinated meat and any extra marinade, cover and cook gently for 40–50 minutes, until the mixture is dry and the chops are cooked.

above: *chops masale vale, lamb pasanda, korma gosht*

Lamb Pasanda

Lamb Curry

Charoli nuts are available from Asian food stores.

500 g (1 lb) lean meat, e.g. boned leg of lamb, cut into thin 2.5 cm (1 inch) strips
150 g (5 oz) natural yogurt
3–4 garlic cloves, crushed
20 g (¾ oz) piece of fresh root ginger, peeled and crushed, or 1 teaspoon ground ginger
1 teaspoon ground coriander
1½ teaspoons ground cumin
25 g (½ oz) ground almonds or ground charoli nuts
1 teaspoon garam masala
25–40 g (1–1½ oz) ghee or 2–3 tablespoons oil
250 g (8 oz) onions, finely chopped
125 ml (4 fl oz) water (optional)
3–4 green chillies, halved and deseeded, or 1 teaspoon chilli powder
lemon juice
salt
To garnish:
chopped coriander leaves
flaked almonds

Put the meat, yogurt, garlic, ginger, coriander, cumin, almonds or charoli nuts, garam masala and a pinch of salt into a large bowl. Mix together well, cover and leave to marinate for 1 hour.

Heat the ghee or oil in a large frying pan and fry the onions until light brown. Add the marinated meat and fry until well browned. Cover and cook over a gentle heat for 40–45 minutes until the meat is tender. If the mixture becomes too dry before the meat is cooked add the water. Add the chilli halves, or chilli powder, and continue cooking for 5–8 minutes.

Sprinkle with lemon juice and garnish with chopped coriander leaves and almonds. Serve with pulao rice and bread.

Serves 4

Korma Gosht

Meat Curry

25 g (1 oz) ghee or 2 tablespoons oil
1 onion, sliced
2 bay leaves
2.5 cm (1 inch) cinnamon stick
about 8 peppercorns
8–10 cloves
4 small green cardamoms
2 large cardamoms
500 g (1 lb) meat, e.g. lamb or stewing steak, cubed
4–5 garlic cloves, crushed
15 g (½ oz) piece of fresh root ginger, peeled and crushed, or 1 teaspoon ground ginger
about 25–50 g (1–2 oz) ground almonds (optional)
about 1 teaspoon chilli powder
½ teaspoon ground turmeric
1½ teaspoons ground cumin
1½ teaspoons ground coriander
150 g (5 oz) natural yogurt
300 ml (½ pint) water
10 g (¼ oz) creamed coconut
salt
edible silver leaf (varak), to garnish

Heat the ghee or oil in a large pan and fry the onion until light brown. Add the bay leaves, cinnamon, peppercorns, cloves, small and large cardamoms, and continue frying for 30 seconds. Add the cubed meat and stir in the garlic, ginger, ground almonds, if using, chilli powder, turmeric, cumin, coriander and salt. Fry for about 7 minutes until the meat is fairly dry and the oil or ghee separates and rises to the surface. Stir in the yogurt and fry gently to remove the moisture. Add the water, cover and cook over a gentle heat for 40–45 minutes, or until the meat is tender. Stir in the creamed coconut for the last 5–10 minutes of cooking. Garnish with edible silver leaf.

Serves 4

Rogan Josh

Rich Lamb with Almonds

This is a very special dish which is often made for special occasions such as weddings and feasts. It is sometimes decorated with edible beaten silver leaf known as *varak*.

50 g (2 oz) ghee or 4 tablespoons oil
125 g (4 oz) onion, finely chopped
5 small green cardamoms
½ teaspoon ground turmeric
about 1 teaspoon chilli powder
1 teaspoon ground cumin
1½ teaspoons paprika
1 teaspoon ground coriander
150 g (5 oz) natural yogurt
½ x 225 g (7½ oz) can tomatoes, finely chopped
625 g (1¼ lb) boned leg of lamb, cut into 2.5 cm (1 inch) cubes
salt
coriander leaves, to garnish

Masala:

15 g (½ oz) piece of fresh root ginger, peeled
6–7 garlic cloves
1 mace blade
¼ teaspoon grated or ground nutmeg
4 cloves
1 tablespoon poppy seeds, dry roasted (optional)
12 peppercorns
50 g (2 oz) almonds, blanched
2 large cardamoms
pinch of saffron threads (optional)

To make the masala, grind the ginger, garlic, mace, nutmeg, cloves, poppy seeds, peppercorns, almonds, large cardamoms and saffron with a little water to make a fine paste.

Heat the ghee or oil in a saucepan and gently fry the onion until light brown. Add the small green cardamoms and stir in the spice paste. Fry gently for 2 minutes, taking care not to burn the mixture. Add the turmeric, chilli powder, cumin, paprika and coriander and fry for a further 1–2 minutes. Stir in the yogurt and the chopped tomatoes. Add the lamb and salt to taste and stir well.

Cover and cook over a gentle heat for 40–50 minutes, sprinkling with a little water if necessary. Garnish with coriander leaves. Serve with pulao or fried rice.

Serves 4

Dum Ka Raan

Dry Spiced Roast Lamb

In India a *dum* is cooked by heat from above and below. This is done by covering the container lid with hot cinders and cooking the pot over a wood or charcoal fire.

150 g (5 oz) piece of fresh root ginger, peeled
8–10 garlic cloves
2 green chillies, deseeded and roughly chopped
2 teaspoons cumin seeds
20 cloves
1 teaspoon peppercorns
3 large cardamoms
8 small green cardamoms
3–4 coriander sprigs
3 tablespoons lemon juice
1 tablespoon vinegar
150 g (5 oz) natural yogurt
about ½ teaspoon chilli powder
2 teaspoons ground coriander
2 teaspoons paprika
1.75–2 kg (3½–4 lb) lean leg of lamb
oil or fat, for roasting
2.5 cm (1 inch) cinnamon stick
2 bay leaves
salt

To garnish:

lime slices
mint sprigs
onion rings

left: *rogan josh*
above right: *dum ka raan*

Put the ginger, garlic, green chillies, cumin seeds, cloves, peppercorns, large and small cardamoms, and coriander leaves into a spice grinder and grind to a paste with a little water. Mix the paste with the lemon juice, vinegar and yogurt and add the chilli powder, coriander and paprika.

Make regular 2.5 cm (1 inch) deep cuts across the meat and sprinkle with salt. Rub in the spice mixture, cover and leave for at least 40–50 minutes, turning the meat from time to time and rubbing in any surplus spices.

To roast the meat, heat the oil or fat in a roasting tin. Add the meat, the marinade, cinnamon and bay leaves and cook in a preheated oven, 220°C (425°F), Gas Mark 7, for 30 minutes to seal in the juices.

Reduce the oven temperature to 200°C (400°F), Gas Mark 6, cover the meat with foil and continue cooking for 1–1½ hours, or until the meat is tender. Baste the meat with the marinade from time to time Discard the marinade and carve. Garnish with lime, mint and onion rings.

Serves 4

Variation: Alternatively pot roast the lamb. Heat 150–175 g (5–6 oz) fat or oil in a flameproof casserole or heavy saucepan. Brown the meat quickly all over in the hot fat. Add the marinade, cinnamon and bay leaves, cover tightly and cook over a very low heat for about 1–1½ hours until tender. Turn the lamb over once or twice and baste during cooking. Sprinkle with a little water if necessary.

Calcutta Beef

1 teaspoon salt
2 teaspoons chilli powder
2 teaspoons ground coriander
1 teaspoon pepper
1½ teaspoons ground turmeric
1 teaspoon ground cumin
1 litre (1¾ pints) milk
1 kg (2 lb) braising steak, cubed
125 g (4 oz) ghee
2 large onions, thinly sliced
5 garlic cloves, thinly sliced
7.5 cm (3 inch) piece of fresh root ginger, peeled and thinly sliced
2 teaspoons garam masala

Place the salt, chilli powder, coriander, pepper, turmeric and cumin into a large bowl. Mix in a little of the milk to make a paste, then gradually add the remaining milk. Add the beef and turn until well coated.

Melt the ghee in a large saucepan, add the onions, garlic and ginger and fry gently for 4–5 minutes until soft. Remove the beef from the spice mixture, add to the pan and fry, turning the meat to seal.

Increase the heat, add the spice mixture and bring to the boil. Cover, reduce the heat and cook gently for 1½–2 hours until the beef is tender and the sauce reduced.

Just before serving, sprinkle in the garam masala. Increase the heat and boil until the sauce is thick. Transfer to a warmed serving dish and serve.

Serves 4–6

Boti Kebabs

Although these kebabs are best cooked in a charcoal oven, a *tandoor*, or barbecued over charcoal they can be cooked under the grill or in the oven.

25 g (1 oz) piece of fresh root ginger, peeled and ground to a paste
1 garlic clove, crushed
500 g (1 lb) boned leg or shoulder of lamb, cut into thin 2.5 cm (1 inch) lengths
1½ teaspoons chilli powder
2 tablespoons vinegar
1 teaspoon pepper
juice of 1 lemon
salt
a little oil
To garnish:
lemon slices
coriander sprig

In a large bowl mix the ginger and garlic with the meat. Sprinkle with the chilli powder, vinegar, pepper and salt. Mix well to coat the meat with the spices. Add the lemon juice, cover and leave to marinate for 3–4 hours or overnight.

Before cooking, stir the marinated ingredients again, then thread the pieces of meat on to skewers. Place the kebabs on a flameproof tray and put them under a preheated grill for about 4–5 minutes on each side, brushing them with a little oil occasionally. Serve garnished with lemon slices and coriander.

Serves 4

Variation: These kebabs may also be cooked in the oven. Arrange the kebabs on a wire rack in a baking tin and cook them in a preheated oven, 180°C (350°F), Gas Mark 4, for 15–20 minutes, turning the kebabs so they cook evenly.

Chops Mirchwala

Pork Chops in Chilli Sauce

8 garlic cloves
15 g (½ oz) piece of fresh root, peeled, or 2 teaspoons ground ginger
1 tablespoon vinegar
about 1½ teaspoons chilli powder
8 small pork chops, trimmed of excess fat
salt
a little oil, for brushing

Grind the garlic, ginger with the vinegar to make a thick paste. Add the chilli powder, mix well and rub the mixture over the chops. Cover and set aside for 30–40 minutes or leave overnight in a refrigerator.

Sprinkle the chops with salt, brush them with oil, then place them in a casserole dish. Cover and cook in a preheated oven, 180°C (350°F), Gas Mark 4, for 40–45 minutes, turning the chops a few times, until well cooked.

Serves 4

Shami Kebabs

500 g (1 lb) lean meat, cubed, e.g. boned leg of lamb
1 small onion, sliced
2.5 cm (1 inch) cinnamon stick
1 bay leaf
150 g (5 oz) chickpeas
1 small egg, beaten
2 teaspoons garam masala
1 tablespoon ground almonds or charoli nuts
1 teaspoon pepper
salt
oil, for frying
Filling:
½ small onion, finely chopped
5 g (¼ oz) piece of fresh root ginger, peeled and finely chopped
1 coriander sprig, chopped
1 green chilli, deseeded and very finely chopped (optional)
2 teaspoons lemon juice or natural yogurt

Put the meat into a large saucepan and cover with water. Add the sliced onion, cinnamon, bay leaf and chickpeas, cover and simmer for about 50–60 minutes until dry and the meat is very tender. Remove the cinnamon stick and bay leaf.

Put the meat mixture into a food processor or blender and work to the consistency of sausagemeat. Add the egg, garam masala, nuts, pepper and salt. Mix well and set aside.

To make the filling, put the finely chopped onion, ginger, chopped coriander, chilli, lemon juice or yogurt and a pinch of salt in a bowl

and mix well. Take a small portion of the meat paste and make a hollow in the middle. Put about ¼ teaspoon of the filling in the hollow and pat the meat paste into a round flat shape to enclose the filling. Continue to make the rest of the kebabs in the same way.

Heat the oil in a frying pan and shallow-fry the kebabs for 2–3 minutes on each side until golden brown.

Makes 10–12

above: *boti kebabs, chops mirchwala, shami kebabs*

Dam Ke Kababs

Dry Baked Kebabs

500 g (1 lb) lean minced beef or lamb
½ large onion, finely chopped
2 teaspoons finely grated fresh root ginger
2 garlic cloves, crushed
about 1 teaspoon chilli powder
½ teaspoon ground turmeric
½ large onion, sliced
salt
oil, for frying
To garnish:
green chillies, deseeded and very finely chopped
chopped fresh root ginger
chopped coriander leaves
lemon wedges
raw onion rings

In a bowl, mix the minced meat, the finely chopped onion, ginger, garlic, chilli powder, turmeric and salt. Stir well, then cover and leave for at least 2–3 hours or overnight if possible in the refrigerator.

Heat the oil and fry the sliced onion until golden brown. Remove with a slotted spoon and set aside. Mix the fried onion with the marinated ingredients and spread the mixture in a greased baking dish. Level the surface and brush with a little oil. Cook in a preheated oven, 180°C (350°F), Gas Mark 4, for 40–45 minutes, by when the mixture should be fairly dry.

Serve garnished with the chopped chillies, ginger, coriander leaves, lemon wedges and onion rings.

Serves 4

Tomatar Gosht

Meat with Tomatoes

50 g (2 oz) ghee or 4 tablespoons oil
1 onion, chopped
25 g (1 oz) piece of fresh root ginger, peeled and crushed
4–5 garlic cloves, crushed
½ teaspoon ground turmeric
1 teaspoon ground coriander
1½ teaspoons ground cumin
500 g (1 lb) braising steak or leg of lamb, cut into cubes
1–2 green chillies, deseeded and finely chopped, or 1 teaspoon chilli powder
400 g (13 oz) can tomatoes
2–3 coriander sprigs, chopped
salt
sliced tomato, to garnish

Heat the ghee or oil in a pan and fry the onion until light brown. Add the ginger, garlic, turmeric, coriander, cumin, the meat and salt to taste. Mix together well, then cover and cook over a gentle heat for 10–12 minutes. Add the chillies, or chilli powder, the tomatoes and coriander leaves. Cover and cook for a further 50 minutes. Garnish with sliced tomato and serve with rotis, naan or parathas.

Serves 4

Meat Madras

Madras is the main city of southern India and famous for many unique dishes, the special flavour of which comes from coconut and curry leaves.

50 g (2 oz) ghee or 4 tablespoons oil
1 small onion, chopped
500 g (1 lb) lean lamb or beef, cut into cubes
150–175 ml (5–6 fl oz) water
1 tablespoon coriander seeds
10 peppercorns
2 cm (¾ inch) cinnamon stick
3 cloves
½ teaspoon chilli powder
1 medium onion, chopped
125 g (4 oz) fresh coconut, grated, or 65 g (2½ oz) desiccated coconut
5–6 curry leaves
½ teaspoon ground turmeric
salt

Heat 40 g (1½ oz) of the ghee or 3 tablespoons of the oil in a large pan and fry the small onion until light brown. Add the meat and water, cover and cook gently for 20–25 minutes until the meat is fairly tender. Remove from the heat and stir until the softened onion is thoroughly incorporated.

In a separate pan, dry roast the coriander, peppercorns, cinnamon, cloves and chilli powder over a gentle heat for a few seconds, without letting them burn. Allow to cool and grind to a fine powder.

Heat the remaining ghee or oil and fry the medium onion until light brown. Add the coconut and curry leaves and cook for 30 seconds, then add the turmeric, ground spices, salt and the cooked meat mixture. Cook for about 20 minutes until the meat is tender and the sauce has thickened, adding a little extra water if the mixture becomes too dry.

Serve as a main dish with pulao rice or parathas.

Serves 4

Goan Meat Curry

50 g (2 oz) ghee or 4 tablespoons oil
1 onion, chopped
5 small garlic cloves, chopped
500 g (1 lb) lean lamb or beef, cut into small pieces
5 garlic cloves, ground to a paste
25 g (1 oz) piece of fresh root ginger, peeled and ground to a paste
3 green chillies, deseeded and very finely chopped
½ teaspoon ground turmeric
2 teaspoons aniseed powder
40 g (1½ oz) creamed coconut, roughly chopped

right: *from bottom left, Goan meat curry, tomator gosht, meat Madras*

about 250 ml (8 fl oz) water
2–3 coriander sprigs, chopped
salt
lemon slices, to garnish (optional)

Heat the ghee or oil in a large pan and fry the onion and chopped garlic until the onion is light brown. Add the meat, the garlic and ginger paste, chopped chillies and turmeric and mix well. Fry for 6–7 minutes until the meat is dry. Sprinkle on the aniseed powder, add salt to taste, then stir in the creamed coconut and fry for 1–2 minutes. Add the water and coriander leaves.

Cover the pan and cook gently for 30–40 minutes, or until the meat is tender. Garnish with lemon slices if liked and serve with rice.

Serves 4

Kofte Ka Salan

Curried Meatballs

500 g (1 lb) lean minced meat
1 teaspoon garam masala
½ teaspoon ground ginger
1 small garlic clove
1 teaspoon ground cumin
Sauce:
25–40 g (1–1½ oz) ghee or 2–3 tablespoons oil
1 onion, chopped
2.5 cm (1 inch) cinnamon stick
4 small green cardamoms
1 bay leaf
4 cloves
1 teaspoon grated fresh root ginger or ground ginger
1 garlic clove, crushed
about 1 teaspoon chilli powder
1 teaspoon ground coriander
¼ teaspoon ground turmeric
150 g (5 oz) natural yogurt
about 600 ml (1 pint) water
salt

Mix together the mince, the garam masala, ginger, garlic and cumin and set aside.

To make the sauce, heat the ghee or oil in a large pan and fry the onion until light brown. Add the cinnamon, cardamoms, bay leaf and cloves and fry for 1 minute. Remove from the heat and stir in the ginger and garlic, chilli powder, coriander and turmeric.

Return the spice mixture to the heat and fry gently for 30 seconds. Add the yogurt and salt. Cover and cook until the mixture is dry and the ghee or oil separates from the spice mixture and rises to the surface. Gradually stir in the water, cover the pan and simmer the sauce for 10–12 minutes.

Shape the reserved meat mixture into 16–20 small balls and slide them, one at a time, into the sauce. Cover and simmer gently for 30–40 minutes. The thickness and quantity of the gravy can be adjusted by adding more water or reducing the excess liquid.

Serves 4

Variation: This recipe can be used as the basis for *Nargisi kofta*, which resembles Scotch eggs. Hard-boil 10–12 small eggs and allow them to go cold. Use the meat mixture to coat the eggs and gently fry them in a little oil until the outside is lightly browned. Prepare the sauce as in the main recipe and carefully slide the meatballs into the sauce and cook as before.

above: *kofte ka salan*
right: *keema*

Keema

Dry Mince Curry

Popular as a breakfast dish eaten with with *parathas*, *keema* is also used to fill *samosas* and for *biryani*. It is usually cooked until dry.

25 g (1 oz) ghee or 2 tablespoons oil
1 onion, chopped
2.5 cm (1 inch) cinnamon stick
4 small green cardamoms
2 large cardamoms
1 bay leaf
500 g (1 lb) lean minced beef or lamb
¼ teaspoon ground turmeric
about 1 teaspoon chilli powder
1 teaspoon ground coriander
1½ teaspoons ground cumin
150 g (5 oz) natural yogurt or 225 g (7½ oz) can tomatoes
125 g (4 oz) frozen peas (optional)
salt

To garnish (optional):
chopped coriander leaves
1 green chilli, deseeded and very finely chopped

Heat the ghee or oil in a large pan and fry the onion until light brown. Add the cinnamon, small and large cardamoms, and the bay leaf. Continue frying for 1 minute.

Add the minced beef or lamb and sprinkle with the turmeric, chilli powder, coriander and cumin. Mix well and fry for 2–3 minutes to brown the meat, then add the yogurt or tomatoes, and salt. Cover and gently cook for about 10 minutes until the mince is dry. Remove the lid, add the peas, if using, and continue cooking over a gentle heat for 10 minutes.

Serve garnished with coriander leaves and chilli if liked.

Serves 4

Coriander Beef with Aubergine

75 ml (3 fl oz) oil
2 onions, finely sliced
2.5 cm (1 inch) piece of fresh root ginger, chopped
3 garlic cloves, chopped
3 tablespoons ground coriander
½ teaspoon hot chilli powder
1 kg (2 lb) lean boneless beef, cut into 4 cm (1½ inch) cubes
475 ml (16 fl oz) beef stock
1 large aubergine, cut into 4 cm (1½ inch) cubes
750 g (1½ lb) tomatoes, chopped
400 g (13 oz) can chickpeas, drained
1 teaspoon garam masala
salt and pepper

Heat the oil in a large saucepan, add the onions and cook for 5 minutes until tender. Add the ginger, garlic, coriander and chilli powder, then cook for 2 minutes. Stir in the beef and brown for 5 minutes, turning frequently.

Add the stock and bring to the boil. Reduce the heat, cover the pan and simmer for 1½ hours.

Stir in the aubergine, cover and simmer for 20 minutes. Add the tomatoes and chickpeas, cover and simmer for a further 10 minutes, then season to taste with salt and pepper. Stir in the garam masala and serve at once.

Serves 6

Apricot and Lamb Curry

4 onions, 2 quartered and 2 chopped
2 garlic cloves
½–1 teaspoon small dried red chillies
50 g (2 oz) blanched almonds
1 tablespoon ground coriander
3 tablespoons oil
5 cm (2 inch) cinnamon stick
6 cardamom pods
8 cloves
750 g (1½ lb) boned leg of lamb, cubed
300 g (10 oz) natural yogurt
250 g (8 oz) dried apricots, soaked overnight
1 tablespoon chopped mint, plus a sprig to garnish
salt

Purée the quartered onions, garlic, chillies, almonds and coriander in a liquidizer or food processor.

Heat the oil, add the cinnamon, cardamoms and cloves and quickly fry, discard when they change colour. Add the chopped onions and fry until soft. Add the paste and fry for 3–4 minutes. Add the lamb and fry, stirring, for 5 minutes. Stir in the yogurt, a little at a time, then the apricots and salt. Simmer, partially covered, for 40 minutes until tender. Stir in the mint and serve garnished with the mint sprig.

Serves 4

***left:** apricot and lamb curry*

Palak Gosht

Meat with Spinach

1 kg (2 lb) fresh spinach, trimmed, washed and chopped, or 500 g (1 lb) frozen leaf spinach, defrosted and chopped
50 g (2 oz) ghee or 4 tablespoons oil
1 small onion, sliced
40 g (1½ oz) piece of fresh root ginger, peeled and crushed
5 garlic cloves, crushed
1 teaspoon chilli powder
1 teaspoon ground coriander
1 teaspoon ground cumin
4 fresh tomatoes, skinned and roughly chopped
½ teaspoon ground turmeric
500 g (1 lb) boned leg or shoulder of lamb, cut into small cubes
200 ml (7 fl oz) water
salt

If using fresh spinach, place it in a saucepan with the water that clings to the leaves and cook until wilted, then strain. Either sieve or blend the fresh or frozen spinach to make a purée and set aside.

Heat the ghee or oil in a large pan and fry the onion until light brown. Add the ginger, garlic, chilli powder, coriander and cumin and fry gently for 1–2 minutes. Add the tomatoes, turmeric and salt. Continue frying gently for 10–15 minutes, until the ghee or oil separates and rises to the surface. Add the meat and cook for 7 minutes, or until the meat is dry.

Add the water, cover and cook gently for 30–40 minutes. After about 15 minutes and when the sauce has been reduced by half, add the spinach purée. Stir well, cover the pan and simmer gently for the remaining 15–20 minutes.

Serves 4–6

Shahi Korma

Royal Lamb Curry

1 kg (2 lb) boneless lamb, cubed
juice of 1 lemon
250 g (8 oz) natural yogurt
75 g (3 oz) ghee
2 onions, sliced
4 garlic cloves, sliced
2.5 cm (1 inch) piece of fresh root ginger, sliced
7.5 cm (3 inch) cinnamon stick
10 cloves
10 cardamom pods
2 teaspoons ground coriander
2 teaspoons ground cumin
2 teaspoons chilli powder
1 teaspoon ground turmeric
300 ml (½ pint) boiling water
125 g (4 oz) blanched almonds
50 g (2 oz) shelled pistachios
150 ml (¼ pint) single cream
salt and pepper

Mix the lamb in a bowl with the lemon juice and yogurt then cover and leave to marinate for 2 hours.

Heat the ghee in a large saucepan, add the onions, garlic and ginger and fry for 5 minutes. Add the cinnamon, cloves and cardamoms and fry for 1 minute. Add the coriander, cumin, chilli powder, turmeric and salt and pepper and cook for 2–3 minutes. Add the lamb and marinade, then stir in the boiling water. Stir in half of the almonds, cover and simmer for 50 minutes.

Add the remaining almonds, pistachios and cream and simmer for 5–10 minutes without boiling. Serve hot.

Serves 6

Note: *Varak* (edible silver leaf) is often used to decorate this rich and exotic curry. It is safe to eat and aluminium foil should not be used as a substitute.

Chicken

Murgh Ka Salan

Chicken Curry

40 g (1½ oz) ghee or 3 tablespoons oil
1 large onion, chopped
2.5 cm (1 inch) cinnamon stick
6 cloves
1–2 bay leaves
4–6 small green cardamom pods
2 teaspoons black cumin (optional)
1 .5–1.75 kg (3–3½ lb) oven-ready chicken, cut into 8 pieces
25 g (1 oz) piece of fresh root ginger, peeled and ground to a paste
1½ garlic cloves, crushed
1–2 teaspoons chilli powder
½ teaspoon ground turmeric
2 teaspoons ground cumin
150 g (5 oz) natural yogurt
450 ml (¾ pint) water
salt
To garnish:
chopped coriander leaves
green pepper slices

Heat the ghee or oil in a large frying pan and fry the onion until light brown. Stir in the cinnamon, cloves, bay leaves, cardamoms and black cumin, if using, and fry for 1–2 minutes. Add the chicken and fry for 1–2 minutes.

Stir in the ginger, garlic, chilli powder, turmeric and ground cumin and fry for 1–2 minutes, then add the yogurt and salt. Cover and cook for about 10 minutes until the moisture has evaporated.

When the ghee or oil separates from the mixture and rises to the surface, stir in the water. Cover and cook gently for 30–40 minutes or until the chicken is tender. Taste and adjust the seasoning and add extra water or reduce the sauce, if necessary.

Garnish with chopped coriander and green pepper slices. Serve as a main dish with rice and bread.

Serves 8

above: *murgh ka salan*
right: *murgh tomatar*

Murgh Tomatar

Tomato Chicken Curry

40 g (1½ oz) ghee or 3 tablespoons oil
1 onion, sliced
2.5 cm (1 inch) cinnamon stick
4 small green cardamoms
2 green chillies, halved and deseeded
50 g (2 oz) piece of fresh root ginger, peeled and finely sliced
6–7 garlic cloves, sliced
1.5–1.75 kg (3–3½ lb) oven-ready chicken, cut into 8 pieces
2 teaspoons ground cumin
3–4 coriander sprigs, chopped
400 g (13 oz) can tomatoes
salt

Heat the ghee or oil in a very large saucepan and fry the onion until light brown. Add the cinnamon, cardamoms and green chillies and fry for 1 minute, then add the sliced ginger and garlic and fry for a further 30 seconds. Add the chicken pieces and fry for 10–15 minutes.

Add the cumin and the coriander leaves and fry for 1–2 minutes, then stir in the tomatoes and salt. Cover and cook over a gentle heat for 30–35 minutes until the chicken is tender.

Serves 8

Pineapple Chicken Curry

2 onions, quartered
2 garlic cloves
3.5 cm (1½ inch) piece of fresh root ginger, peeled and chopped
1 teaspoon ground turmeric
1 tablespoon ground coriander
1–2 teaspoons chilli powder
2 tablespoons paprika
1 teaspoon sugar
1 teaspoon salt
2 tablespoons oil
8 chicken thighs, skinned
300 ml (½ pint) water
125 g (4 oz) cashew nuts, soaked in boiling water for 1 hour
6 curry leaves
4 green chillies, slit
1 medium pineapple, cubed
juice of ½–1 lemon

Purée the onions, garlic, ginger, turmeric, coriander, chilli powder, paprika, sugar and salt in a food processor until smooth.

Heat the oil in a saucepan, add the spice paste and fry for 10 minutes. Add the chicken pieces and fry for 5 minutes. Pour in the water and bring to simmering point. Add the drained nuts, curry leaves and chillies, cover and simmer for 25 minutes. Add the pineapple and lemon juice to taste and simmer gently for a further 10 minutes. Serve hot.

Serves 4

Murgh Makhanwalla

Butter Chicken

1.5–1.75 kg (3–3½ lb) oven-ready chicken, cut into 8 pieces
1 tablespoon lemon juice
1 green chilli, deseeded and roughly chopped
5 g (¼ oz) piece of fresh root ginger, peeled
3 small garlic cloves
150 g (5 oz) natural yogurt
2 teaspoons paprika
¼ teaspoon chilli powder
orange food colouring (optional)
a little melted butter
175 g (6 oz) unsalted butter
150 ml (¼ pint) soured cream
salt

With a sharp knife, make regular slits through the skin and flesh of the chicken pieces. Rub with salt, then sprinkle with the lemon juice.

Grind the green chilli, ginger and garlic to a fine paste. Mix the paste with the yogurt, paprika, chilli powder and a few drops of orange food colouring, if using. Place the chicken pieces in a large bowl and spoon over the spice mixture. Cover and set aside for 4–5 hours to marinate.

Remove the chicken pieces from the marinade, place them in a greased baking dish and cook in a preheated oven, 220°C (425°F), Gas Mark 7, for 45–50 minutes, brushing the chicken pieces with a little melted butter occasionally.

Melt the unsalted butter in a saucepan, add the remaining marinade and the soured cream. Heat gently, without boiling, for 5–6 minutes. Pour the sauce over the baked chicken and serve as a main dish with naan bread.

Serves 8

Variation: Add 50 g (2 oz) finely chopped cashew nuts or almonds to the simmering sauce.

Goan Chicken Curry

25 g (1 oz) block tamarind
25 g (1 oz) piece of fresh root ginger, peeled
5–6 garlic cloves
10 peppercorns
5 small green cardamoms
6 cloves
2.5 cm (1 inch) cinnamon stick
2 tablespoons vinegar
40 g (1½ oz) ghee or 3 tablespoons oil
1 large onion, sliced
1.5–1.75 kg (3–3½ lb) oven-ready chicken, cut into 8 pieces
½ teaspoon ground turmeric
1–1½ teaspoons chilli powder
400 ml (14 fl oz) water

50 g (2 oz) creamed or desiccated coconut or fresh coconut, grated
1 teaspoon sugar (optional)
few curry leaves (optional)
salt
slices of green pepper, to garnish

Break up the tamarind and soak in 125 ml (4 fl oz) boiling water for 10–15 minutes then press through a sieve to extract as much liquid as possible. Discard the pulp.

Grind the ginger, garlic, peppercorns, cardamoms, cloves and cinnamon with the vinegar to make a fine paste.

Heat the ghee or oil in a large pan and fry the onion until light brown. Add the chicken pieces and fry for 5–6 minutes to brown them lightly. Add the spice paste, turmeric and chilli powder, and fry for a further 1–2 minutes, then add the water and simmer gently.

Add the coconut, the tamarind liquid, salt, sugar and curry leaves, and stir well. Cover and cook for about 45 minutes, or until the chicken is tender.

Garnish with green pepper and serve as a main dish with rice.

Serves 8

left: murgh makhanwalla
right: tandoori chicken

Tandoori Chicken

1.5–1.75 kg (3–3½ lb) oven-ready chicken, cut into 8 pieces
about 1 teaspoon chilli powder
1 teaspoon pepper
5 g (¼ oz) piece of fresh root ginger, peeled and ground to a paste
3 garlic cloves, ground to a paste
2 teaspoons paprika
300 g (10 oz) natural yogurt
1 tablespoon lemon juice
orange food colouring (optional)
salt
oil, for brushing

With a sharp knife, make regular slits through the skin and flesh of the chicken pieces. Rub with salt. Mix together the chilli powder, pepper, ginger, garlic, paprika, yogurt, lemon juice and a few drops of orange food colouring, if using. Put the chicken pieces into a large bowl and spoon over the tandoori paste. Cover and set aside to marinate for 10–12 hours. The longer it is left the better the result will be.

Place the chicken pieces on a grill pan and cook them under a preheated hot grill for about 15 minutes on each side, turning them regularly and brushing with oil occasionally.

Serve with a fresh crisp salad.

Serves 8

Variation: These chicken portions may also be baked in the oven. Arrange them on a wire rack in a baking dish and cook in a preheated oven, 220°C (425°F), Gas Mark 7, for 35–45 minutes, or until the juices run clear when pierced with a skewer. Brush the chicken with oil occasionally and brown evenly.

Chicken Molee

- 3 tablespoons oil
- 4 boneless, skinless chicken breasts, diced
- 6 cardamom pods
- 6 cloves
- 5 cm (2 inch) cinnamon stick
- 1 large onion, sliced
- 2 garlic cloves
- 4 cm (1½ inch) piece of fresh root ginger, peeled and chopped
- 3 green chillies, deseeded
- juice of 1 lemon
- 1 teaspoon ground turmeric
- 50 g (2 oz) creamed coconut
- 150 ml (¼ pint) hot water
- salt

To garnish:

- red pepper slices
- herb sprigs

Heat the oil in a pan, add the chicken and fry quickly to brown all over. Remove with a slotted spoon.

Add the cardamoms, cloves and cinnamon and fry for 1 minute. Add the onion and fry until soft.

Purée the garlic, ginger, chillies and lemon juice in a food processor or blender. Add to the pan with the turmeric and cook for 5 minutes.

Melt the coconut in the hot water and add to the pan with salt to taste. Simmer for 2 minutes then add the chicken and any juices. Simmer for 15–20 minutes, until tender, then garnish with the red pepper slices and herb sprigs and serve at once.

Serves 4

Chicken Korma

- 175 g (6 oz) natural yogurt
- 2 teaspoon ground turmeric
- 3 garlic cloves, sliced
- 1.5 kg (3 lb) oven-ready chicken
- 125 g (4 oz) ghee
- 1 large onion, sliced
- 1 teaspoon finely chopped fresh root ginger
- 5 cm (2 inch) cinnamon stick
- 5 cloves
- 5 cardamom pods
- 1 tablespoon crushed coriander seeds
- 1 teaspoon ground cumin
- ½ teaspoon chilli powder
- 1 teaspoon salt
- 1½ tablespoons desiccated coconut
- 2 teaspoons roasted almonds

***above:** chicken molee*
***right:** chicken pilau*

Put the yogurt, turmeric and 1 of the garlic cloves in a food processor or liquidizer and purée to mix evenly. Place the chicken in a dish and pour over the yogurt mixture. Cover and chill in the refrigerator overnight.

Melt the ghee in a saucepan, add the onion and the remaining garlic and fry gently for 4–5 minutes until soft. Add the ginger, cinnamon, cloves, cardamoms, coriander, cumin, chilli powder and salt and fry for a further 3 minutes, stirring constantly.

Add the chicken with the yogurt marinade and the coconut and turn the chicken in the marinade to coat it well. Cover and simmer for 1¼–1½ hours until the chicken is tender. Transfer to a warmed serving dish and scatter with the almonds.

Serves 4

Note: This dish may be cooked more quickly if the chicken is cut into pieces before marinating. Simmering time would then be about 45 minutes.

Chicken Pilau

In a meat or chicken pilau the meat is cooked with the spices before the rice is added. The use of saffron is expensive, but it really does enhance the flavour and appearance of the dish.

375 g (12 oz) basmati rice
1.5–1.75 kg (3–3½ lb) oven-ready chicken
5 tablespoons ghee or butter
5 cm (2 inch) cinnamon stick
8 cloves
6 cardamom seeds
2 garlic cloves, crushed
½–1 teaspoon chilli powder
1 tablespoon fennel seeds
5 tablespoons natural yogurt
1 teaspoon powdered saffron
1½ teaspoons salt
about 600 ml (1 pint) chicken stock
fried onion rings, to garnish

Wash the rice thoroughly and soak it in cold fresh water for 30 minutes; drain. Skin the chicken and cut it into pieces.

Melt the ghee or butter in a large flameproof casserole. Add the cinnamon, cloves and cardamoms and fry for 30 seconds. Stir in the garlic, chilli powder and fennel and fry for 30 seconds. Add the chicken and fry, turning, for 5 minutes. Add the yogurt a spoonful at a time, stirring until absorbed before adding the next spoonful. Cover and simmer for 25 minutes.

Add the rice, saffron and salt. Fry, stirring, until the rice is well mixed. Add enough stock to cover the rice by 5 mm (¼ inch) and bring to the boil. Reduce the heat to very low, cover the casserole tightly and cook for 20 minutes or until the rice is cooked.

Transfer the pilau to a warmed serving dish and garnish with the fried onion rings.

Serves 6

Murgh Mussalam

2 onions
2 garlic cloves
5 cm (2 inch) piece of fresh root ginger, peeled
1 teaspoon poppy seeds
8 peppercorns
300 g (10 oz) natural yogurt
1 teaspoon garam masala
1.75 kg (3½ lb) oven-ready chicken
125 g (4 oz) long-grain rice, soaked in cold water for 1 hour and drained
3 tablespoons ghee
½ teaspoon chilli powder
50 g (2 oz) sultanas
50 g (2 oz) slivered almonds
350 ml (12 fl oz) water
salt
coriander sprigs, to garnish

Put the onions, garlic, ginger, poppy seeds, peppercorns and half the yogurt into a food processor and work to a paste. Stir in the garam masala and add salt to taste. Prick the chicken all over and rub in the blended mixture. Leave for 1 hour.

Heat 1 tablespoon of the ghee in a pan, add the rice and stir-fry for 3 minutes. Add the chilli powder, sultanas, almonds and salt. Pour in half of the water, cover and simmer for about 10 minutes, until the rice is almost tender. Stuff the chicken neck with the cooled rice. Heat the remaining ghee in a large saucepan and add the chicken on its side. Pour in any marinade and the remaining water. Simmer, covered, for 1 hour. Add the remaining yogurt, a spoonful at a time, stirring until it is all absorbed. Cook for a further 15 minutes.

Serves 4

Kashmiri Chicken

125 g (4 oz) butter
3 large onions, finely sliced
10 peppercorns
10 cardamom pods
5 cm (2 inch) cinnamon stick
5 cm (2 inch) piece of fresh root ginger, peeled and chopped
2 garlic cloves, finely chopped
1 teaspoon chilli powder
2 teaspoons paprika
1.5 kg (3 lb) chicken pieces, skinned
250 g (8 oz) natural yogurt
salt
parsley sprigs, to garnish

Melt the butter in a deep, lidded frying pan or wok. Add the onions, peppercorns, cardamoms and cinnamon and fry until the onions are golden. Add the ginger, garlic, chilli powder, paprika and salt to taste and fry for 2 minutes, stirring occasionally.

Add the chicken pieces and fry until browned. Gradually add the yogurt, stirring constantly. Cover and cook for about 30 minutes. Serve hot, garnished with parsley.

Serves 6

Chicken Vindaloo

1.75 kg (3½ lb) oven-ready chicken
250 g (8 oz) ghee
2 large onions, chopped
2 green chillies, cored, deseeded and finely chopped
25 g (1 oz) piece of fresh root ginger, peeled and chopped
3 garlic cloves, chopped
1½ teaspoons ground turmeric
1 teaspoon ground coriander
1 teaspoon garam masala
2 tablespoons malt or cider vinegar
2 curry leaves
300 ml (½ pint) water
1 teaspoon salt
50 g (2 oz) desiccated coconut

Skin and joint the chicken. Heat the ghee in a saucepan and fry the onions and chillies until golden. Add the ginger, garlic, turmeric, coriander and garam masala and fry for a further 3 minutes.

Add the vinegar, curry leaves, water and chicken pieces. Cover and simmer for 30 minutes. Test with a skewer to check that the chicken is cooked. Boil rapidly, uncovered, until the liquid evaporates.

Add the salt and coconut and simmer for 15 minutes.

Serves 4

***right:** murgh mussalam*

Vegetables and Pulses

Gobhi Aloo

Dry Cauliflower and Potato Curry

1 cauliflower
50 g (2 oz) ghee or 4 tablespoons oil
1 onion, peeled and diced or 2 teaspoons cumin seeds
2 potatoes, cut into chunks
about 1 teaspoon chilli powder
½ teaspoon ground turmeric
2 teaspoons ground coriander
2 teaspoons garam masala
2 teaspoons mango powder or juice of 1 lemon
water (optional)
salt
To garnish:
cucumber slices
mint sprigs

Break the cauliflower into florets and cut into medium-sized pieces. Peel away any tough skin and slice the remaining cauliflower stem. Discard the large leaves but retain a few of the tender smaller leaves. Wash the cauliflower pieces and leaves in cold water and drain. Heat the ghee or oil in a saucepan and fry the onion until light brown. Alternatively fry the cumin seeds until they crackle. Add the potatoes and fry for 2–3 minutes, then stir in the cauliflower pieces and leaves and continue frying for about 5 minutes.

Stir in the chilli powder, turmeric, coriander, salt, garam masala and mango powder or lemon juice. Cover and cook gently for 10–15 minutes until the potatoes and cauliflower are tender and the mixture is dry. If necessary add a little water during cooking to prevent the mixture sticking. Avoid stirring the curry during cooking, otherwise the florets will disintegrate. Garnish with cucumber slices and mint sprigs and serve with chapatis.

Serves 4

Sukhi Bandhgobhi

Dry Cabbage Curry

The mixture of seeds used in this dish is known as *panch phoran* and is a speciality of Bengal. It is used for many fish and vegetable dishes, and pickles.

25–40 g (1–1½ oz) ghee or 2–3 tablespoons oil
2 potatoes, cut into chunks
1 bay leaf
500 g (1 lb) cabbage, chopped
about 1 teaspoon chilli powder
½ teaspoon ground turmeric
2 teaspoons ground coriander
1 teaspoon sugar
2.5 cm (1 inch) cinnamon stick
3 small green cardamoms
3 cloves
salt
Panch Phoran:
¼ teaspoon fenugreek seeds
1 teaspoon cumin seeds
½ teaspoon aniseed
½ teaspoon mustard seeds
½ teaspoon onion seeds

To make the panch phoran, mix together the seeds of the five spices in a bowl. Heat the ghee or oil in a large pan and fry the potatoes for 4–5 minutes. Add the panch phoran and the bay leaf and fry for a few seconds. Stir in the cabbage, chilli powder, turmeric, coriander and sugar. Cover and cook gently. Meanwhile, grind the cinnamon stick, cardamoms and cloves to a powder. Alternatively mix ground cinnamon into the powder. Sprinkle on to the cabbage, add salt to taste and mix well. Cover and cook for a further 8–10 minutes or until the potatoes are tender.

Serves 4

__right:__ above, sukhi bandhgobhi, below, gobhi aloo

Masoor Ki Daal

Dry Lentil Curry

250 g (8 oz) red lentils, thoroughly washed
450 ml (¾ pint) water
½ teaspoon ground turmeric
2 teaspoons ground coriander or 3 coriander sprigs, chopped
1 green chilli, halved and deseeded (optional)
2–3 tomatoes, skinned and chopped
6 curry leaves (optional)
50 g (2 oz) clarified butter
1 small onion, diced
salt

Put the lentils and water into a saucepan with the turmeric and coriander and simmer for 15–20 minutes until tender. Mash the lentil mixture with a potato masher. Stir in the green chilli, if using, tomatoes, salt and curry leaves. Cover and simmer gently for about 20–30 minutes. Remove from the heat and set aside.

Heat the butter in a pan and fry the chopped onion until light brown. Serve the daal with the onion mixture poured on top and accompanied by rice or bread.

Serves 4

Variation: To make a sour daal (*khatti daal*), soak 25 g (1 oz) block tamarind in boiling water for 10–15 minutes, then press through a sieve to extract as much liquid as possible. Discard the pulp. Add the tamarind liquid for the last 2–3 minutes cooking time.

Sukhi Tarkari

Dry Mixed Vegetable Curry

25–40 g (1–1½ oz) ghee or
2–3 tablespoons oil
1 small onion, chopped, or
2 teaspoons cumin seeds
500 g (1 lb) diced mixed vegetables (e.g. potatoes, carrots, swede, peas, beans, cauliflower)
about 1 teaspoon chilli powder
2 teaspoons ground coriander
½ teaspoon ground turmeric
2–3 tomatoes, skinned and chopped
300 ml (½ pint) water (optional)
salt

Heat the ghee or oil in a pan and gently fry the onion until light brown. Alternatively fry the cumin seeds until they crackle. Add the diced vegetables, and stir in the chilli powder, coriander, turmeric and salt. Fry for 2–3 minutes.

Add the chopped tomatoes. Stir well and add just a very little water if you prefer a dry vegetable curry. Cover and cook gently for 10–12 minutes until dry. For a moister curry stir in 300 ml (½ pint) water then cover the pan and simmer for 5–6 minutes, until the vegetables are tender.

Serve as a side dish, or as a main dish with rice or chapatis or naan.

Serves 4

above: *sukhi tarkari*
left: *masoor ki daal*
right: *palak aloo*

Palak Aloo

40 g (1½ oz) ghee or butter
250 g (8 oz) potatoes, cut into chunks
2 garlic cloves, crushed
2 teaspoons finely grated fresh root ginger
1 green chilli, halved and deseeded
500 g (1 lb) fresh spinach, chopped
2–3 coriander sprigs, chopped
salt
50 g (2 oz) melted ghee or butter, to serve

Heat the ghee or butter in a pan and fry the potatoes for 4–5 minutes. Add the garlic, ginger and chillies. Fry for 1–2 minutes. Stir in the spinach, chopped coriander and salt. Add a little water and continue frying for 10–15 minutes until the potatoes are tender and the spinach is dry. Serve with melted ghee or butter poured over the top.

Serves 4

Aloo Mattar

Potato, Pepper and Pea Curry

40 g (1½ oz) ghee or 3 tablespoons oil
1 small onion, chopped, or 1½ teaspoons cumin seeds
500 g (1 lb) potatoes, diced
about 1 teaspoon chilli powder
½ teaspoon ground turmeric
1½ teaspoons ground coriander
225 g (7½ oz) can tomatoes
125 g (4 oz) peas
1 green pepper, cored, deseeded and sliced
200 ml (7 fl oz) water
salt
chopped coriander leaves, to garnish (optional)

Heat the ghee or oil in a large saucepan and fry the chopped onion until light brown. Alternatively fry the cumin seeds until they crackle. Add the diced potatoes and fry for about 3–4 minutes. Stir in the chilli powder, turmeric and coriander, and fry for 1–2 minutes.

Add the tomatoes, peas and sliced peppers to the pan, season with salt to taste and stir to mix thoroughly. Cover and cook gently for 1 minute, then stir in the water. Cook until the potatoes are tender. Serve garnished with coriander if liked.

Serves 4

above *aloo mattar*
right: *aloo Madras, dam aloo*

Aloo Madras

Dry Spiced Potato Curry

1 teaspoon cumin seeds
½ teaspoon fenugreek seeds
2 dried red chillies
1 onion, chopped
25 g (1 oz) ghee or 2 tablespoons oil
8–10 curry leaves
1 teaspoon mustard seeds
500 g (1 lb) potatoes, boiled, peeled and cut into chunks
½ teaspoon ground turmeric
1 tablespoon fresh or desiccated coconut
salt

Dry-roast the cumin and fenugreek seeds and chillies in a frying pan for 1 minute. Add the chopped onion and 2 teaspoons of the oil or ghee and continue frying for 1 minute. Grind the mixture with a little water to a fine paste.

Heat the remaining ghee or oil in a pan and add the curry leaves and mustard seeds. Fry for 30 seconds, then add the spice paste, the cooked potatoes, salt, turmeric and fresh or desiccated coconut. Add a little water, cover and cook gently for 3–4 minutes.

Serves 4

Dam Aloo

Dry Potato Curry

500 g (1 lb) small potatoes, preferably new, cut into even-sized pieces
1 onion, roughly chopped
4 tablespoons oil
about 1 teaspoon chilli powder
½ teaspoon ground turmeric
25 g (1 oz) piece of fresh root ginger, peeled and ground to a paste
½ teaspoon sugar
150 ml (¼ pint) water
¼ teaspoon garam masala
salt
coriander sprigs, to garnish

Boil the potatoes until just tender.

Grind the onion to a fine paste. Heat the oil in a pan and fry the onion paste until light brown. Stir in the chilli powder, turmeric, ginger, salt and sugar. Fry for 1–2 minutes without letting the mixture burn, then add the water. When the water begins to simmer, stir in the potatoes, cover and cook until the sauce has thickened. Sprinkle with the garam masala and remove from the heat. Serve, garnished with coriander sprigs.

Serves 4

Baigan Bhurta

Spiced Aubergines

500 g (1 lb) aubergines
40 g (1½ oz) ghee or 3 tablespoons oil
1 large onion, finely chopped
25 g (1 oz) piece of fresh root ginger, peeled and finely chopped
3–4 garlic cloves, chopped
about 1 teaspoon chilli powder
½ teaspoon ground turmeric
3–4 coriander sprigs, chopped
1 green chilli, deseeded and very finely chopped (optional)
4–5 tomatoes, skinned and chopped
salt

Prick the aubergines with a fork or skewer and put them under a preheated grill for about 15 minutes, turning them frequently until the flesh feels soft. Leave to cool then squeeze out the juice. Scrape off the burnt skin with a knife and chop the flesh.

Heat the ghee or oil in a saucepan and gently fry the onion until just tender. Add the chopped ginger and garlic. Fry for 1–2 minutes, then add the chopped aubergine. Stir in the chilli powder, turmeric, chopped coriander, chopped chilli, salt and tomatoes. Fry for 10–15 minutes until dry. Serve with chapatis.

Serves 4

Lehsun Baigan

40 g (1½ oz) ghee
2 potatoes, cut into chunks
4–5 garlic cloves, lightly crushed
500 g (1 lb) aubergines, cubed and put in salted water
about ½ teaspoon chilli powder
½ teaspoon ground turmeric
1½ teaspoons ground coriander
salt
coriander sprigs, to garnish

Heat the ghee in a saucepan and fry the potatoes for 5–6 minutes. Add the garlic and continue frying until the garlic is golden brown.

Drain and dry the aubergine cubes and add them to the pan then stir in the chilli powder, turmeric, coriander and salt. Add a little water, cover and cook gently for 8–10 minutes until the potato is tender. Do not stir too vigorously as the aubergine will disintegrate. Serve, garnished with coriander.

Serves 4

Ghassey

Dry Chipped Potatoes with Garlic

500 g (1 lb) potatoes, preferably new, scrubbed but not peeled
4–5 garlic cloves, lightly crushed
40 g (1½ oz) ghee or 4 tablespoons oil
2 teaspoons urid daal or lentil flour
5–6 curry leaves
3 red or green chillies
salt

Cut the potatoes into very thin 2.5 cm (1 inch) long chips. Wash thoroughly and drain and dry well.

Heat the ghee or oil in a pan and gently fry the garlic until light brown. Add the urid daal and the curry leaves and fry gently for 30 seconds. Add the whole red or green chillies and fry for about 15 seconds.

Add the chipped potatoes, season with salt, and mix well. Cover and fry gently for 10–12 minutes until the chips are tender, turning them occasionally. If necessary a little water may be added during cooking. If preferred remove the garlic before serving.

Serve with daal and rice, or parathas and rotis.

Serves 4

Baigan Tamatar

Aubergines with Tomatoes

750 g (1½ lb) aubergines, sliced
juice of 1 lemon
175 g (6 oz) ghee
2 onions, thinly sliced
4 garlic cloves, thinly sliced
7.5 cm (3 inch) piece of fresh root ginger, peeled and thinly sliced
2 teaspoons black onion seeds
7.5 cm (3 inch) cinnamon stick
2 teaspoons coriander seeds
2 teaspoons cumin seeds
2 teaspoons garam masala
1½ teaspoons ground turmeric
1 teaspoon chilli powder
400 g (13 oz) can tomatoes
125 g (4 oz) tomato purée
600 ml (1 pint) boiling water
salt and pepper

Sprinkle the aubergines with 1 tablespoon salt, put them in a colander and leave to drain for 30 minutes. Rinse the aubergines and pat dry with kitchen paper. Place in a bowl and mix with the lemon juice.

Heat the ghee in a large saucepan, add the onions, garlic and ginger and fry gently for 4–5 minutes until soft. Add the onion seeds, cinnamon, coriander and cumin and stir well. Fry for a further 2 minutes, then stir in the salt, pepper, garam masala, turmeric and chilli powder. Add the tomatoes with their juice, and the tomato purée, stir well and bring to the boil. Add the boiling water, aubergines and lemon juice. Bring to the boil, then simmer gently for 15–20 minutes until soft.

Serves 4–6

far left: *lehsun baigan*
above left: *baigan bhurta*
left: *ghassey*

Lundey Ka Salan

Egg Curry

25 g (1 oz) ghee or 2 tablespoons oil
2 onions, chopped
2.5 cm (1 inch) cinnamon stick
1 garlic clove, crushed
1 teaspoon finely chopped fresh root ginger
about 1 teaspoon chilli powder
1 teaspoon ground cumin
1½ teaspoons ground coriander
1 teaspoon garam masala
225 g (7½ oz) can tomatoes, chopped
300 ml (½ pint) water
2 teaspoons cornflour blended with a little water (optional)
8 hard-boiled eggs, shelled
salt
celery leaves or coriander, to garnish

Heat the ghee or oil in a saucepan and gently fry the onions. Add the cinnamon and stir for a few seconds. Stir in the garlic, ginger, chilli powder, cumin, coriander and garam masala and continue frying gently for 30 seconds. Add the tomatoes and salt. Fry for about 5 minutes until the mixture is very thick. Stir in the water and if necessary add the cornflour to thicken. Carefully add the eggs, cover and simmer gently for 8–10 minutes. Garnish with celery leaves or coriander and serve.

Serves 4

Aloo Gajjar

Dry Carrot and Potato Curry

15–25 g (½–1 oz) ghee or 1–2 tablespoons oil
2 teaspoons cumin seeds
250 g (8 oz) carrots, diced
250 g (8 oz) potatoes, diced
about 1 teaspoon chilli powder
½ teaspoon ground turmeric
1 teaspoon ground coriander
125 ml (4 fl oz) water
salt
mint sprigs, to garnish

Heat the ghee or oil in a pan and fry the cumin seeds until they crackle. Add the carrots and potatoes and continue frying for 5–6 minutes. Add the chilli powder, turmeric, coriander, salt and the water. Cover and cook for about 5–7 minutes until the carrots and potatoes are tender and the mixture is dry. To serve, garnish with mint sprigs.

Serves 4

***above right:** aloo gajjar, daalcha*
***left:** lundey ka salan*

Daalcha

Pulses with Meat and Vegetables

In this recipe the meat should be left on the bone and chopped. Ideally ask your butcher to do this for you. It is important to use split chickpeas (*chana daal*) rather than the whole variety which take longer to cook.

40 g (1½ oz) block tamarind
25–40 g (1–1½ oz) ghee or 2–3 tablespoons oil
1 onion, diced
2.5 cm (1 inch) cinnamon stick
1 garlic clove, crushed
1 teaspoon finely chopped fresh root ginger
375 g (12 oz) meat, e.g., breast of lamb, trimmed and cut into pieces
about 1 teaspoon chilli powder
1 teaspoon ground cumin
½ teaspoon ground turmeric
2–3 tomatoes, skinned and sliced
1.2 litres (2 pints) water
8–10 curry leaves
150 g (5 oz) split chickpeas
250 g (8 oz) courgettes, sliced
1 green chilli, deseeded and very finely chopped
2–3 coriander sprigs, chopped (optional)
salt

Break up the tamarind and soak in 175 ml (6 fl oz) boiling water for 10–15 minutes then press through a sieve to extract as much liquid as possible. Discard the pulp.

Heat the ghee or oil in a large pan and fry the onion until light brown. Fry the cinnamon, garlic, ginger, and the meat for 4–5 minutes. Stir in the chilli powder, cumin, turmeric and tomatoes and continue frying for a few minutes. Add the tamarind liquid, 750 ml (1¼ pints) of the water, curry leaves and salt. Cover the pan and simmer gently for 50–60 minutes until the meat is cooked.

Meanwhile, bring the remaining 450 ml (¾ pint) of water to the boil, add the chickpeas and cook for 20–30 minutes until tender. Mash the mixture and set aside. When the meat is cooked, stir in the chickpea daal and the courgette slices, and continue simmering until the courgettes are tender and the sauce is fairly thick. Add the chopped chilli and coriander leaves.

Serves 4

Makkai

Dry Spiced Sweetcorn

40 g (1½ oz) ghee or
3 tablespoons oil
1 small onion, chopped
1 potato, cubed
2 green chillies, halved and deseeded
5–6 curry leaves
175 g (6 oz) sweetcorn
about ½ teaspoon chilli powder
1 teaspoon ground coriander
225 g (7½ oz) can tomatoes
2–3 coriander sprigs, chopped
1 teaspoon garam masala
lemon juice, to taste
salt

Heat the ghee or oil in a pan and fry the onion until just tender. Add the potato and fry for 4–5 minutes. Add the chillies and curry leaves, fry for 1–2 minutes, then stir in the sweetcorn, chilli powder, coriander and turmeric and fry for 3–5 minutes until the curry is dry.

Add salt and the tomatoes, cover and cook for 5–8 minutes, until the potatoes are tender and the sauce has thickened. Stir in the chopped coriander, garam masala and lemon juice to taste.

Serves 4

above: *lentil coconut curry,*
right: *from the top, makkai, shaljam ki tarkari, kaddu*

Lentil Coconut Curry

40 g (1½ oz) butter
3 onions, finely chopped
2 garlic cloves, finely chopped
1 tablespoon grated fresh root ginger
2–4 green chillies, finely chopped
1 teaspoon ground turmeric
250 g (8 oz) moong daal lentils, washed and drained
1.2 litres (2 pints) water
50 g (2 oz) creamed coconut
juice of 1 lemon
salt
finely sliced green chilli rings, to garnish

Melt the butter in a large saucepan, add the onions, garlic, ginger and chillies and fry gently, stirring, until the onions are soft.

Stir in the turmeric and immediately add the daal. Fry, stirring, for 1 minute. Pour in the water, add salt to taste and bring to the boil, then partially cover the pan and simmer gently for 40 minutes.

Add the coconut and stir until dissolved, then stir in the lemon juice. Taste and adjust the seasoning if necessary, then cover the pan and simmer for 10 minutes.

Transfer to a warmed serving dish and garnish with the chilli rings.

Serves 4

Kaddu

Pumpkin Curry

500 g (1 lb) pumpkin
20 g (¾ oz) tamarind block
40 g (1½ oz) ghee or 3 tablespoons oil
¼ teaspoon cumin seeds
¼ teaspon mustard seeds
¼ teaspoon fenugreek seeds
¼ teaspoon onion seeds
¼ teaspoon aniseed
3 potatoes, cut into chunks
about 1 teaspoon chilli powder
½ teaspoon ground turmeric
1 teaspoon ground coriander
1 teaspoon sugar
salt

Peel the pumpkin in alternate strips so as to keep the flesh intact during cooking, and cut it into cubes. Wash and drain well.

Break up the tamarind and soak in 75 ml (3 fl oz) boiling water for 10–15 minutes then press through a sieve to extract as much liquid as possible. Discard the pulp.

Heat the ghee or oil in a pan and fry the cumin, mustard, fenugreek and onion seeds and aniseed for 30 seconds, then add the potatoes and fry for 2–3 minutes. Add the pumpkin cubes, stir well and fry for 4–5 minutes.

Stir in the chilli, turmeric, coriander, salt and sugar and continue frying for 5–6 minutes. Add the tamarind liquid, cover and cook until the potatoes are tender. Add 1 tablespoon water to the mixture during the cooking if necessary.

Serves 4

Shaljam Ki Tarkari

Dry Turnip Curry

500 g (1 lb) turnips
50 ml (2 fl oz) boiling water
50 g (2 oz) ghee or 75 g (3 oz) butter
1 onion, sliced
1 green chilli, deseeded and very finely chopped
1 teaspoon garam masala
about ¼ teaspoon sugar (optional)
juice of 1 lemon
salt

Slice the turnips into rounds and cook in the boiling water until tender and dry.

Heat the ghee or butter in a pan and fry the onion until light brown. Add the chopped chilli, turnips, garam masala and salt. Taste and add sugar if liked. Cook for about 5 minutes.

Serve as a side dish sprinkled with lemon juice.

Serves 4

Breads and Rice

Roti

Flat Bread

This bread does not contain any fat in the dough, instead it is brushed with melted *ghee* or butter after it has been cooked. The dough will keep in a refrigerator for up to a week.

500 g (1 lb) plain wholemeal flour
about 125–175 ml (4–6 fl oz) water
salt
melted butter or ghee, for brushing

Sift the flour and a pinch of salt into a bowl. Make a well in the centre and gradually add enough water to make a soft dough. Knead well until no longer sticky.

Shape the dough into 24 small balls. On a floured surface, roll out each ball into an 18 cm (7 inch) round. Gently heat a frying pan or Indian bread pan and place a round of dough in it. When little brown specks appear on the underside, turn the round over and cook briefly on the other side. Flip the roti over again and with a clean tea towel, press gently to circulate steam all around, until the underside is golden brown. Cook the other side in the same way. Remove and place on a plate. Brush melted ghee or butter over the top of the roti and keep wrapped in a tea towel, or place in a covered container. Cook the remaining rotis and stack them in a pile one on top of the other.

Makes 24

Variations: A mixture of plain white and wholemeal flour may be used.

Rogani Roti

Rich Bread

Rogan means creamy and *rogani roti* is made with milk and butter or cream. This type of bread is usually soft and keeps well for a few days. In India it is often given to elderly people who may find it difficult to eat the firmer breads. *Rogani roti* also makes good use of any leftover cream.

500 g (1 lb) plain wholemeal flour
150 ml (¼ pint) milk
50 g (2 oz) butter or 50 ml (2 fl oz) cream
ghee or butter, for frying (optional)
salt

Mix the flour and a pinch of salt in a bowl and make a well in the centre. Warm the milk slightly and melt the butter in it, but do not allow the milk to boil. Gradually add the milk, and butter or cream, to the flour. Knead well for 1–2 minutes.

Divide the dough into 22–24 portions. On a lightly floured surface roll one portion into a 12–15 cm (5–6 inch) round about 5 mm (¼ inch) thick.

Gently heat a frying pan or Indian bread pan and put the dough round into it. Cook the dough on both sides over a moderate heat until brown specks appear. Then either press the roti with a clean tea towel or add 1 teaspoon ghee or butter to the pan and cook briefly until golden brown on both sides. Remove the roti from the pan and wrap it in a tea towel, or place in a covered container to keep warm. Cook the rest of the rotis in the same way and stack them one on top of the other.

Makes 22–24

Variation: A combination of yogurt and cream, or all soured cream, or evaporated milk may be used instead of the milk mixture.

A mixture of plain white flour and wholemeal flour may be used.

right: *from the top, paratha (see page 63), rogani roti, roti*

Naan Bread

½ teaspoon dried yeast
1 teaspoon sugar
125 ml (4 fl oz) lukewarm milk or water
500 g (1 lb) plain white flour
½ teaspoon salt
1 teaspoon baking powder
1 tablespoon natural yogurt
25 g (1 oz) ghee or butter
sesame seeds (optional)
melted ghee or butter, for brushing

Stir the yeast and sugar into the milk or warm water and leave covered for 10–15 minutes in a warm place until the liquid is frothy.

Sift the flour, salt and baking powder into a bowl and make a well in the centre. Add the yogurt and ghee or butter and mix to make a soft dough, gradually adding the yeast solution, and a little extra milk or water if necessary. Cover and set aside for 4–5 hours.

Knead the dough well for 1–2 minutes. Divide it into 18–20 balls and roll them out on a floured surface. Brush the shapes with the melted ghee or butter and sprinkle with sesame seeds. Place on greased baking sheets and cook in a preheated oven, 190°C (375°F), Gas Mark 5, for 3–4 minutes on both sides until brown specks appear.

Makes 18–20

left: naan bread

Paratha

Shallow-fried Bread

Paratha are brushed with melted *ghee* or butter and then shallow-fried. Sometimes they have a meat or vegetable filling. They can be triangular, square or round. The dough will keep in a refrigerator for up to a week.

500 g (1 lb) plain wholemeal flour
about 125–175 ml (4–6 fl oz) water
salt
melted ghee or butter, for brushing

Mix the flour and a pinch of salt in a bowl and make a well in the centre. Gradually add enough water to make a soft dough and knead well until it is no longer sticky. Divide into 16 pieces.

On a floured surface, roll each piece into a flat round and brush ghee or butter all over the surface. Fold in half and brush with ghee or butter and fold again into a small triangle. Roll out thinly with a little extra flour. Alternatively, to make round parathas roll each piece into a 13–15 cm (5–6 inch) round and brush with ghee or butter. then fold in a little at one edge and roll each piece into a tube shape. Hold the shape upright and flatten it into a ball. Roll out thinly with a little extra wholemeal flour.

Gently heat a frying pan or Indian bread pan and place a piece of dough in it. Cook on each side for 1–2 minutes. Brush 1 teaspoon melted ghee or butter over the surface, turn the shape over and fry gently until golden brown. Repeat with the second side. Remove from the pan and keep wrapped in a tea towel, or place in a covered container. Cook the remaining parathas and stack them one on top of the other.

Makes 16

Variations: To make stuffed *paratha*, roll one piece into a ball and make a hollow in the middle. Press about one teaspoon of a dry mince curry (such as Keema on page 37), or a dry vegetable curry, into the hollow and shape the dough into a ball to enclose the filling. Carefully roll out into a 7.5 cm (3 inch) circle. Fill the remaining pieces in the same way and fry them as in the main recipe.

Grated raw cauliflower, onions or radishes can be used as fillings, seasoned with salt, chilli powder and ground cumin seeds, to taste.

Puri

Deep-fried Bread

When frying *puris* there are two important points to remember. One, the oil should be the right temperature and, two, the second side needs frying longer so that the *puri* swells up.

500 g (1 lb) plain wholemeal flour
1 teaspoon salt
about 125–175 ml (4–6 fl oz) water
oil, for deep-frying

Mix the flour and salt in a bowl and make a well in the centre. Gradually add the water to make a dough. Knead well for 1–2 minutes then set aside, covered, for 5 minutes.

Divide the dough into 25–28 pieces. Roll each one into a flat 7 cm (3 inch) round.

Heat 5–6 cm (2–2½ inches) oil in a deep frying pan and drop a small amount of flour into the oil. If it floats to the surface and turns light brown the oil is at the correct temperature. Slide in 1 puri at a time and fry on both sides until light brown. It will quickly swell up in the oil.

Lift our the puri with a slotted spoon and drain on kitchen paper. Continue frying the puris and stack one on top of the other, alternating the thin and thick sides so as to prevent sticking. Keep the puris wrapped in a tea towel or put them in a covered container.

To keep puris warm for a longer period, wrap them in foil and put them in a container. If puris are left uncovered they become crisp, and unsuitable for eating with curries.

Makes 25–28

Variations: Add either 1 teaspoon onion seeds, or ½ teaspoon chilli powder to the dough or, to make green *puris*, add 2 tablespoons spinach purée.

About 25 g (1 oz) *ghee* may be mixed into the dough to make softer *puris*.

Use a mixture of wholemeal and plain white flour.

Kachori

Stuffed Deep-fried Bread

500 g (1 lb) plain wholemeal flour
½ teaspoon salt
125–175 ml (4–6 fl oz) water
Urid daal filling:
125 g (4 oz) urid daal, washed and soaked for 3 hours
1 teaspoon cumin seeds
1 teaspoon aniseed
2 tablespoons oil
pinch of asafoetida (optional)
1 green chilli, deseeded and very finely chopped, or 1 teaspoon chilli powder
pinch of salt
oil, for deep-frying

Sift the flour and salt into a bowl and make a well in the centre. Gradually add the water to make a dough. Knead well for 1–2 minutes, then cover and set aside.

To make the urid daal filling, drain the urid daal and grind it to a thick coarse paste with a little water. Dry roast the cumin seeds and aniseed for 30 seconds then grind coarsely. Heat the oil in a pan and sprinkle in the asafoetida, if using, and urid daal mixture. Sprinkle with the chilli, salt and ground spices. Fry for 5 minutes, adding a little extra oil if necessary. Leave to cool.

Divide the dough into 25–28 pieces. Roll one piece into a ball and make a hollow in the middle. Press about 1 teaspoon of the filling into the hollow and shape the dough into a ball to enclose the filling. Carefully roll out into a 7 cm (3 inch) circle. Make the remaining kachoris in the same way.

Heat 5–6 cm (2–2½ inches) oil in a deep frying pan and fry the kachoris a few at a time until golden brown on both sides. Keep warm. Serve warm with a chutney or tomato ketchup.

Makes 25–28

Variations: To make green pea kachoris, lightly mash 125 g (4 oz) uncooked peas and 15 g (½ oz) chopped fresh root ginger and use instead of the *urid daal* filling.

right: *puri, green pea kachori, kachori*

Poppadoms

Poppadoms, which make an excellent nibble to serve with drinks, as well as with Indian meals, are usually bought ready-made and heated in a frying pan. However, this recipe for making them from scratch is included for interest. *Urid daal* or lentil flour is sold in Indian supermarkets and specialist shops.

500 g (1 lb) urid daal or lentil flour
4½ teaspoons salt
1 tablespoon baking powder
250 ml (8 fl oz) lukewarm water
about 50 g (2 oz) ghee
2 teaspoons black peppercorns
vegetable oil, for frying

Sift the flour, salt and baking powder into a mixing bowl and gradually add the water to form a very hard dough.

Melt the ghee. Knead the dough for at least 20 minutes, sprinkling it with enough melted ghee to prevent it sticking. Crush the peppercorns and sprinkle them over the dough, then knead until evenly distributed.

Break the dough into about 20 pieces and roll them out very thinly until they are 15 cm (6 inches) in diameter. Stack on top of each other between sheets of greaseproof paper, then dry them in a preheated oven, 180°C (350°F), Gas Mark 4, for 2–2 ½ hours.

To cook, heat the oil in a deep frying pan until hot. Add the poppadoms, two at a time and fry for about 5–10 seconds, then turn them over and cook for a further 5–10 seconds (frying two together prevents them from curling up). Drain on kitchen paper.

Makes about 20

Prawn and Spinach Rice

500 g (1 lb) long-grain basmati rice
½ teaspoon ground turmeric
50 g (2 oz) butter
3 tablespoons oil
2 onions, sliced
3 garlic cloves, finely chopped
1 tablespoon grated fresh root ginger
1–2 teaspoons chilli powder
2 teaspoons ground coriander
1 kg (2 lb) fresh spinach, chopped
500 g (1 lb) peeled prawns
salt

Wash the rice thoroughly under cold running water. Leave to soak for 30 minutes in cold water, then drain. Fill a large saucepan two-thirds full with water and bring to the boil. Add the rice, 1 teaspoon salt and the turmeric. Boil for 3 minutes, then drain. Stir the butter into the rice.

Heat the oil in a large pan, add the onions, garlic and ginger and fry until golden. Stir in the chilli powder, coriander and 1 teaspoon salt and fry for a few seconds. Add the spinach and cook, stirring, until soft. Stir in the prawns.

Layer the spinach and prawns with the buttered rice in an ovenproof casserole, beginning and ending with spinach. Cover tightly and bake in a preheated oven, 180°C (350°F), Gas Mark 4, for 30 minutes. Serve hot.

Serves 4

Saffron Rice

175 g (6 oz) ghee
2 large onions, sliced
375 g (12 oz) long-grain basmati rice
1 teaspoon cloves
4 cardamom pods
1 teaspoon salt
1 teaspoon pepper
½ teaspoon saffron threads, soaked in 1 tablespoon boiling water for 30 minutes
750 ml (1¼ pints) boiling water
silver leaf (varak), to garnish (optional)

Melt the ghee in a large saucepan, add the onions and fry gently for 4–5 minutes until soft.

Wash the rice thoroughly under cold running water. Leave to soak for 30 minutes in cold water, then drain. Add to the pan with the cloves, cardamoms, salt and pepper, then fry for 3 minutes, stirring frequently. Add the saffron with its liquid and stir well to mix. Add the water and bring to the boil. Lower the heat and simmer for 15–20 minutes until the rice is cooked. Drain. Transfer to a warmed serving dish and garnish with the silver leaf, if using. Serve hot.

Serves 4

far left: *poppadoms*
left: *prawn and spinach rice*

Biryani One

There are two ways of cooking a *biryani*. Both are easy and produce the unique result required. In the first method, the meat and rice are cooked separately, then layered in a pan and heated through together. A simple *raita*, salad or chutney is often the only accompaniment needed but in restaurants a curry sauce is sometimes served as a side dish.

75 g (3 oz) ghee or butter
1 onion, sliced
1 bay leaf
1 cm (½ inch) cinnamon stick
4 small green cardamom pods
2 large cardamom pods
6 cloves
500 g (1 lb) meat, cubed
2 teaspoons finely grated fresh root ginger
2 garlic cloves, crushed
½ teaspoon ground turmeric
2 teaspoons ground coriander
2 teaspoons ground cumin
150 ml (¼ pint) natural yogurt
1 teaspoon salt
about 1 teaspoon chilli powder
450 ml (¾ pint) water

To cook the rice:
750 g (1½ lb) long-grain basmati rice, rinsed and drained
2.5–2.75 litres (4–5 pints) water
2 teaspoons salt
1 bay leaf
1 cm (½ inch) cinnamon stick
1 teaspoon black cumin seeds

To finish:
1 small onion, sliced and fried
3–4 coriander sprigs, chopped
2 green chillies, deseeded and very finely chopped
4 small green cardamom pods, ground
juice of 2 lemons
yellow food colouring or a pinch of powdered saffron dissolved in water
3 tablespoons milk
25 g (1 oz) ghee or butter
pepper
coriander sprigs
green chilli slices

Melt the ghee or butter in a large saucepan and fry the onion until golden. Add the bay leaf, cinnamon, cardamoms and cloves. Fry for 1 minute. Add the meat, ginger, garlic, turmeric, coriander, cumin, yogurt, salt and chilli powder, and stir well. Cover and cook until dry.

Increase the heat and fry until the oil separates from the mixture. Add the water and continue cooking for 40–50 minutes until the meat is tender. There should be about 3 tablespoons thick sauce.

Meanwhile, cook the rice. Place it in a large saucepan, add the water, salt, bay leaf, cinnamon and black cumin seeds. Bring to the boil and cook the rice until it is almost tender. Remove from the heat and drain thoroughly.

Put a thin layer of rice in the bottom of a clean, heavy-based pan. Spread over a layer of cooked meat, without the sauce, followed by layers of fried onion, chopped coriander leaves and chillies. Repeat the layers once or twice, retaining a little onion and chopped coriander and finishing with a layer of rice.

Sprinkle the top with fried onion, chopped coriander, pepper, cardamom and the lemon juice. With a spoon handle, make three or four holes in the rice to allow the steam to rise, and pour the food colouring or saffron, the remaining

left: *biryani one*
right: *biryani two*

sauce, milk and ghee or butter at random over the surface. Place the pan over a moderate heat and as soon as any steam is visible, lower the heat, cover the pan and cook very gently for 5 minutes.

To serve, garnish with coriander sprigs and chilli slices.

Serves 4

Biryani Two

In this method, known as *kachhi handi ki biryani*, the rice is partially cooked then added to the marinated meat and cooked with it.

125 g (4 oz) ghee or butter
1 onion, sliced
1 cm (½ inch) cinnamon stick
1 bay leaf
4 small green cardamom pods
2 large cardamom pods
6 cloves
2 garlic cloves, crushed
2 teaspoons finely grated fresh root ginger
about 1 teaspoon chilli powder
2 teaspoons ground cumin
2 teaspoons ground coriander
½ teaspoon ground turmeric
500 g (1 lb) meat, cubed
150 ml (¼ pint) natural yogurt
1 teaspoon salt

To cook the rice:

2.5–2.75 litres (4–5 pints) water
750 g (1½ lb) long-grain basmati rice, rinsed and drained
1 teaspoon black cumin seeds
1 cm (½ inch) cinnamon stick
1 bay leaf

To finish:

1 small onion, sliced and fried
chopped coriander leaves
2 green chillies, halved and deseeded
2 tablespoons milk
4 small green cardamom pods, ground
juice of 2 lemons
yellow food colouring or a pinch of ground saffron dissolved in water
pepper

Melt the ghee or butter in a pan and fry the onion until golden brown. Add the cinnamon, bay leaf, cardamoms and cloves and fry for 1 minute. Remove from the heat. Stir in the garlic, ginger, chilli powder, cumin, coriander, turmeric, meat, yogurt and salt, then cover and set aside.

Meanwhile, pour the water into a large saucepan and add the rice, black cumin seeds, cinnamon, bay leaf and salt to taste. Bring to the boil and cook for 5–7 minutes until the rice is half cooked. It should still feel firm but have soaked up some water. Drain well.

Transfer the meat mixture to a large ovenproof casserole and level the surface. Spread the rice evenly on top. Sprinkle with the fried onion, half of the chopped coriander, the green chillies, lemon juice and milk. Make three or four holes with a spoon handle to allow the steam to rise, and pour the food colouring or saffron at random over the surface. Cover and cook in a preheated oven, 160°C (325°F), Gas Mark 3, for 50–60 minutes. When both the rice and meat are cooked, mix them together before serving. Garnish the dish with the remaining chopped coriander.

Serves 4

Variation: Add a few drops of rosewater or kewra water for flavouring, stirred in with the food colouring.

Sada Pulao

Plain Fried Rice

Plain fried rice is eaten in one form or another all over the Asia. The rice is usually cooked in oil flavoured with a garam masala and cumin seeds or onion. When rice is cooked with fish, meat and poultry it is called a *pulao* or *biryani*, with pulses it is called *khichhari*, and when combined with vegetables it is called a *tahiri* or *pulao*.

375 g (12 oz) long-grain basmati rice
75 g (3 oz) ghee or butter
1 small onion, chopped
1 teaspoon salt
750 ml (1¼ pints) water

Wash the rice thoroughly under cold running water. Leave to soak for 30 minutes in cold water, then drain well.

Melt the ghee or butter in a large pan and fry the chopped onion until golden brown. Add the rice and salt, and fry for 1 minute.

Add the water, cover and bring to the boil. Lower the heat and gently stir the rice a few times. Cover and cook on a very gentle heat for 10–15 minutes until the water is fully absorbed and the rice is cooked. Do not stir during the cooking. If the rice is not cooked by the time the water is fully absorbed, add 1 tablespoon water and continue cooking until the rice is tender.

Serves 4

Variations: Add 1 teaspoon black cumin seeds or a garam masala at the same time as the onion and fry for 1 minute then add the rice. The spices for the garam masala are 4 small green cardamom pods, 2 large cardamom pods, 1 teaspoon black cumin seeds, 4 cloves, 8–10 peppercorns, 1 cm (½ inch) cinnamon stick and 1 bay leaf.

To make egg fried rice, pour 2 beaten eggs over the nearly-cooked rice. Do not stir until the rice is fully cooked and the water absorbed.

left: sada pulao, ubley chawal, pulao gosht (see page 72)

Ubley Chawal

Plain Boiled Rice

This method of cooking rice in a large quantity of water is suitable for every type of rice and produces a fluffy and starch-free result. Lemon juice can be added and this will whiten the rice.

375 g (12 oz) long-grain basmati rice
2.5–2.75 litres (4–5 pints) cold water
½ teaspoon salt
few drops of lemon juice (optional)
melted ghee or butter, to serve (optional)

Wash the rice thoroughly under cold running water. Leave to soak for 30 minutes in cold water, then drain well.

Fill a large saucepan with the cold water. Add the salt, lemon juice, if using, and rice. Bring to the boil and simmer until the rice is almost cooked. The grains should still have a firm centre.

Drain the rice, return it to the pan, then cover the pan and place it over a very low heat for 2 minutes. The moisture left around the rice will be enough to cook the centre of the grains.

Serve the rice as it is or with melted ghee or butter if you prefer.

Serves 4

Pulao Gosht

Meat Pulao

In a meat *pulao* the meat is cooked with spices, then the rice is added. To enhance the appearance and flavour of the dish, nuts, peas or pineapple can be added. A *pulao* may be coloured with a weak orange food colouring solution or with saffron.

500 g (1 lb) long-grain basmati rice
50 g (2 oz) ghee or butter
1 small onion, chopped
1 bay leaf
1 cm (½ inch) cinnamon stick
4 small green cardamom pods
2 large cardamom pods
1 teaspoon black cumin seeds
4 cloves
8 black peppercorns
500 g (1 lb) meat, cubed
about 1 teaspoon salt
1.65 litres (2¾ pints) water

Wash the rice thoroughly under cold running water. Leave to soak for 30 minutes in cold water, then drain well.

Melt the ghee or butter in a large pan and fry the onion until golden brown. Add the bay leaf, cinnamon, cardamoms, cumin, cloves and peppercorns and fry for 1 minute. Add the meat and salt and fry for 2–3 minutes. Stir in the water. Cover the pan and simmer gently for 40–50 minutes until the meat is tender, and the liquid has reduced to about two-thirds its original amount. If the quantity is less than this add a little extra water.

Stir the rice in with the meat and cook on a gentle heat without stirring until the rice is tender and the mixture is dry.

Serves 4

Variations: 125 g (4 oz) of mixed unsalted nuts and raisins, or peas, or potatoes can be added during the cooking, keeping in mind the time it takes for these ingredients to cook. To make a chicken or prawn *pulao* substitute chicken pieces or 250 g (8 oz) peeled prawns for the meat. The prawns will only need to be added to the *pulao* for the last 10–15 minutes of the cooking time.

Tahiri

Vegetable Pulao

Unlike *biryanis pulaos* do not contain hot spices. Although there are various types of *pulao* the flavouring usually comes from onions and a garam masala. All *pulaos* can be coloured by a weak solution of food colouring or by adding ground turmeric or saffron, used sparingly.

375 g (12 oz) long-grain basmati rice
50 g (2 oz) ghee or butter
1 small onion, chopped
50 g (2 oz) frozen peas, thawed
about 1½ teaspoons salt
750 ml (1¼ pints) water

Garam Masala:
4–6 small green cardamom pods
2–3 large cardamom pods
6 cloves
1 bay leaf
1 cm (½ inch) cinnamon stick
1 teaspoon black cumin seeds

Wash the rice thoroughly under cold running water. Leave to soak for 30 minutes in cold water, then drain well.

Melt the ghee or butter in a large saucepan and fry the onion until golden brown. Lower the heat and add the garam masala. Fry for 30 seconds then add the peas. Fry for 1 minute, then add the rice. Sprinkle with the salt and stir gently a few times.

Add the water, bring to the boil and stir briefly. Cover the pan and cook over a very low heat, without stirring, for 10–15 minutes until the water is fully absorbed.

If the rice is not fully cooked by the time the water is fully absorbed add about 1 tablespoon warm water and continue cooking.

Serves 4

***right:** tahiri*

Lime Rice

300 g (10 oz) long-grain basmati rice
600 ml (1 pint) water
2 tablespoons sunflower or mustard blend oil
2 tablespoons unsalted cashews
1 teaspoon black mustard seeds
1 teaspoon sesame seeds
½ teaspoon ground turmeric
1 teaspoon crushed dried curry leaves (optional)
½ teaspoon mango powder (optional)
flesh of ¼ coconut, grated, or 1 tablespoon desiccated coconut
3–4 tablespoons lime juice

Wash the rice thoroughly under cold running water, then soak for about 30 minutes in cold water. Drain well.

Bring the water to the boil in a 3 litre (5 pint) flameproof lidded casserole. Tip the rice into the casserole and stir from time to time until the water returns to the boil. Put the lid on the casserole, turn the heat down to low and cook for 8 minutes.

Meanwhile, heat the oil in a frying pan and fry the cashew nuts for 2 minutes. Add the mustard and sesame seeds, turmeric and curry leaves and mango powder, if using, and fry for 1 minute. Stir the oil, nut and spice mixture into the rice and add the coconut and lime juice.

Put the casserole into a preheated oven, 110°C (225°F), Gas Mark ¼ (the lowest setting), and cook for a minimum of 30 minutes. It can be kept warm for 1–2 hours without spoiling. Just before serving, fluff up the rice with a fork to allow any steam to escape.

Serves 4

Coconut Rice

375 g (12 oz) long-grain basmati rice
450 ml (¾ pint) coconut milk
½ teaspoon ground turmeric
8 shallots, roughly chopped
20 peppercorns
1 teaspoon salt

Wash the rice thoroughly under cold running water. Leave to soak for 30 minutes in cold water, then drain well.

Put the coconut milk into a saucepan, stir in the turmeric, then add the rice. Bring to the boil, then cover and simmer gently for about 10 minutes. Add the shallots, peppercorns and salt and continue cooking gently for another 10 minutes or until the rice is tender. Do not let the rice burn.

Transfer to a warmed serving dish and serve at once.

Serves 4

Raitas and Chutneys

Kakri Raita

Cucumber Raita

250 g (8 oz) natural yogurt
½ cucumber, grated or sliced
1 green or red chilli, deseeded and very finely chopped (optional)
1–2 coriander sprigs, chopped
1 teaspoon pepper
salt
chilli, to garnish

Beat the yogurt in a bowl. Add the cucumber, green or red chilli and chopped coriander, season with salt to taste and the pepper and mix well. Cover and chill until required.

Garnish the raita with a piece of chilli and serve as a side dish with roti and as an accompaniment to a main dish such as a biryani.

Serves 4

above right: *baigan raita*
left: *kakri raita, tarkari ka raita*

Tarkari Ka Raita

Mixed Vegetable Raita

300 g (10 oz) natural yogurt
1–2 teaspoons black pepper or chilli powder
¼ cucumber, diced
1 small onion, diced
1–2 potatoes, boiled, peeled and cubed
2–3 tomatoes, skinned and chopped
125 g (4 oz) radishes, trimmed and sliced
1–2 celery sticks, diced
1 green chilli, deseeded and very finely chopped (optional)
salt
To garnish:
coriander sprigs
radish slices

Beat the yogurt in a bowl with the pepper or chilli powder and salt to taste until smooth. Add the cucumber, onion, potatoes, tomatoes, radishes and celery and mix well. Sprinkle on the green chilli and chill until ready to serve.

Garnish the raita with coriander sprigs and radish slices.

Serves 4

Variations: A dessert apple, cut into cubes, or another fruit may be added.

A little lemon juice can be sprinkled on the raita before serving.

Baigan Raita

Aubergine Raita

oil, for deep-frying
375 g (12 oz) aubergine, sliced into 3 mm (⅛ inch) rounds
300 g (10 oz) natural yogurt
2 teaspoons cumin seeds, dry roasted and coarsely ground
1–2 teaspoons chilli powder
salt

Heat the oil in a deep frying pan and fry the aubergine rounds until golden brown. Lift out with a slotted spoon and drain on kitchen paper. Beat together the yogurt and salt to taste, then pour into a serving dish. Add the fried aubergine and sprinkle with ground cumin and chilli powder.

Serves 4

Variation: Fry and mash the aubergine, and mix with the yogurt. Sprinkle with chopped chilli and coriander leaves.

Boondi Raita

Traditional Raita

Boondi are small fried batter balls and, if preferred, they can be bought ready-made from Asian shops. In this dish they are incorporated into a *raita*.

50 g (2 oz) baisen flour
pinch of baking powder
4–5 tablespoons water
oil, for deep-frying
300 g (10 oz) natural yogurt
1 teaspoon cumin seeds, dry roasted and coarsely ground
salt and pepper
To garnish:
1 green chilli, deseeded and very finely chopped
coriander leaves

Sift the flour and baking powder into a bowl. Gradually beat in enough water to make a thick batter.

Heat the oil in a deep frying pan. Pour a little of the batter on a ladle with holes and quickly shake the ladle over the frying pan so that small drops of the batter fall into the oil. Fry the boondi for 3–4 minutes until crisp, then drain them on kitchen paper. Leave to soften in a little cold water, while frying the remaining boondi. Gently squeeze the boondi to remove most of the water, place in a dish and set aside.

Beat the yogurt, salt and pepper in a bowl. Stir in the boondi.

Sprinkle with the cumin and chill until ready to serve.

Garnish with chopped chilli and coriander leaves and serve with a main dish or with stuffed parathas.

Serves 4

Keley Ki Chutney

Banana Chutney

50–75 g (2–3 oz) block tamarind
2 tablespoons sugar
50 g (2 oz) raisins and sultanas
about 1 teaspoon chilli powder, dry roasted
15 g (½ oz) piece of fresh root ginger, peeled and grated
pinch of salt
2–3 ripe bananas, sliced

1 teaspoon cumin seeds, dry roasted and ground
a little lemon juice or water

Break up the tamarind and soak in 350 ml (12 fl oz) boiling water for 10–15 minutes then press through a sieve to extract as much liquid as possible. Discard the pulp.

In a large bowl mix together the tamarind liquid, sugar, raisins, sultanas and chilli powder and stir until the sugar dissolves. Add the ginger, salt and bananas. Sprinkle with the cumin powder. Add a little lemon juice or water if the chutney is too thick for your taste.

Serves 4

Sev Ki Chutney

Apple Chutney

1.25 kg (2½ lb) cooking apples, peeled and cored
1 tablespoon salt
500 ml (17 fl oz) malt vinegar
300 g (10 oz) soft brown sugar
125 g (4 oz) raisins
125 g (4 oz) sultanas
½ teaspoon mustard seeds
25 g (1 oz) piece of fresh root ginger, peeled and sliced
1–2 garlic cloves, chopped
1 teaspoon chilli powder

above left: *boondi raita*
right: *keley ki chutney, sev ki chutney*

Slice the apples and put them in a dish and sprinkle with half of the salt. Cover and set aside.

Pour half the vinegar into a saucepan, add the sugar and stir over a low heat until the sugar is dissolved. Bring to the boil and boil until a thick syrup has formed. Leave to cool.

Pour the remaining vinegar into a another saucepan, add the apples and simmer for 3–4 minutes until tender. Leave to cool then stir in the vinegar syrup, raisins, sultanas, mustard seeds, salt, chopped ginger, garlic and chilli powder. Bottle in airtight sterilized jars with vinegar-proof tops. Let this chutney mature for 4–5 weeks before using.

Makes about 1.75 kg (3½ lb)

Hari Chutney

Green Chutney

Green chutney is popular in all parts of India. As well as being a good accompaniment to Indian food it can be spread on pieces of bread and made into a delicious sandwich.

50 g (2 oz) block tamarind or 125 g (4 oz) unripe green mango flesh
175 g (6 oz) fresh or desiccated coconut
4–6 large coriander sprigs
1–2 green chillies, deseeded and roughly chopped
25 g (1 oz) piece of fresh root ginger, peeled
1 teaspoon cumin seeds
½–1 teaspoon salt
1 small onion, finely chopped

Break up the tamarind and soak in 300 ml (½ pint) boiling water for 10–15 minutes. Press through a sieve to extract as much liquid as possible. Discard the pulp.

Purée the coconut, coriander leaves, chillies, ginger, cumin seeds and tamarind liquid in a food processor until smooth. If using the mango add a little water. Add the salt and stir in the chopped onion.

Serve with a main dish or with savoury snacks.

Serves 4

above: *hari chutney*
right: *aam ki chutney*

Aam Ki Chutney

Mango Chutney

6 green mangoes
3–4 red chillies, roughly chopped, or
 2 teaspoons chilli powder
300 ml (½ pint) malt vinegar
400 g (13 oz) sugar
25–40 g (1–1½ oz) piece of fresh root
 ginger, peeled and chopped
125 g (4 oz) mixed unsalted nuts and
 raisins, roughly chopped (optional)
salt

Peel the mangoes and grate the flesh into a bowl. Sprinkle with 2 teaspoons of the salt and set aside for 30 minutes.

Grind the red chillies and mix the chillies or chilli powder with a little of the vinegar to make a fine paste. Place the remaining vinegar in a pan, add the sugar and simmer gently, stirring, until the sugar dissolves. Squeeze the grated mangoes with the back of a spoon to extract the juice, and discard. Add the mango flesh to the pan and simmer gently for a further 5–6 minutes. Add the ginger and the chilli paste and mix well. Cook for 10–12 minutes.

Taste and add a pinch of salt. Stir in the chopped nuts and raisins and cook for 4 minutes. Remove from the heat and leave to cool. Bottle in sterilized airtight jars with vinegar-proof tops.

Makes about 1.25 kg (2½ lb)

Variation: Add 2 teaspoons dry roasted cumin seeds, 2 teaspoons ground coriander and 250 g (8 oz) dessert dates during cooking.

Apricot Chutney

250 g (8 oz) ready-to-eat dried
 apricots
150 ml (¼ pint) vinegar
250 g (8 oz) sugar
25 g (1 oz) piece of fresh root ginger,
 peeled and crushed
about 1 teaspoon chilli powder
salt

Place the apricots in a saucepan with water to cover. Simmer until tender then blend in a food processor until smooth. Put the vinegar, sugar, ginger, chilli powder and a pinch of salt in another pan and heat gently, stirring, until the sugar has dissolved, then increase the heat until a syrup is formed.

Stir the apricot purée into the syrup and simmer for about 10 minutes to the desired thickness. Leave to cool then bottle in sterilized airtight jars with vinegar-proof tops until ready to use.

Serves 4–6

Tarkari Ki Chutney

Mixed Vegetable Chutney

25 g (1 oz) block tamarind
2 tablespoons oil
1 teaspoon mustard seeds
1 small onion, diced
1 sweet potato, diced (optional)
1 carrot, diced
50 g (2 oz) sweetcorn kernels
1 kg (2 lb) tomatoes, skinned and chopped
1 teaspoon salt
about 1 teaspoon chilli powder
½ teaspoon ground turmeric
50 g (2 oz) piece of fresh root ginger, peeled and grated
3 tablespoons soft brown sugar
200 ml (7 fl oz) malt vinegar
125 g (4 oz) sultanas
125 g (4 oz) raisins
75 ml (3 fl oz) water
½ cucumber, chopped and squeezed dry

Break up the tamarind and soak in 125 ml (4 fl oz) boiling water for 10–15 minutes then press through a sieve to extract as much liquid as possible. Discard the pulp.

Heat the oil in a pan and fry the mustard seeds. When they begin to crackle add the onion, sweet potato, carrot and sweetcorn and fry for 4–5 minutes. Add the tomatoes, salt and chilli powder, cover and simmer until the tomatoes are soft.

Stir in the turmeric, grated ginger, sugar, vinegar, tamarind liquid, raisins and sultanas. Simmer gently until the sugar syrup is thick and the vegetables are tender, adding a little water if necessary. Add the cucumber and simmer for 1 minute. Leave to cool. Store in the refrigerator and eat within 7 days.

Makes about 1 kg (2 lb)

Hara Dhania Chutney

Coriander Chutney

50 g (2 oz) block tamarind or
150 g (5 oz) natural yogurt
1 small onion, sliced (optional)
8–10 large coriander sprigs, stalks discarded
25 g (1 oz) piece of fresh root ginger, peeled and chopped
2 teaspoons cumin seeds
5–6 mint sprigs
1½–2 tablespoons sugar
1–2 green chillies,deseeded and roughly chopped
½ teaspoon salt

If using tamarind break it into pieces and soak in 175 ml (6 fl oz) boiling water for 10–15 minutes then press through a sieve to extract as much liquid as possible. Discard the pulp. Place all the ingredients in a food processor and blend until smooth. Taste and add more sugar or salt if necessary.

Serves 4

right: above, til copra chutney, below, hara dhania chutney
left: tarkari ki chutney, apricot chutney (see page 79)

Til Copra Chutney

Sesame Seed and Onion Chutney

125 g (4 oz) block tamarind
125 g (4 oz) sesame seeds, dry roasted
125 g (4 oz) desiccated coconut
1 green chilli, deseeded and roughly chopped
3–4 coriander sprigs, stalks discarded
1 teaspoon salt
1 onion, thinly sliced
a little water or lemon juice (optional)

Break up the tamarind and soak in 750 ml (1¼ pints) boiling water for 10–15 minutes then press through a sieve to extract as much liquid as possible. Discard the pulp. Purée the sesame seeds, coconut, chilli, coriander and tamarind liquid to a smooth paste. Add the salt and stir in the sliced onion. If the chutney is too thick add a little water or lemon juice or a mixture of both.

Serve as a condiment or spread on slices of bread to make sandwiches.

Serves 4

Desserts and Drinks

Spiced Semolina Dessert

250 g (8 oz) semolina
4 tablespoons desiccated coconut
500 g (1 lb) sugar
1 tablespoon poppy seeds
seeds of 6 cardamom pods
600 ml (1 pint) water
125 g (4 oz) ghee, melted

Place the semolina in a large saucepan with the coconut, sugar, poppy and cardamom seeds. Mix well together, then stir in the water. Bring to the boil, stirring constantly, then lower the heat and simmer for at least 1 hour, stirring frequently, until all the ingredients are soft. Gradually add the ghee and mix well.

Transfer the mixture to a shallow tray and spread evenly. Leave to cool, then cut into triangles, diamond shapes, or a shape of your choice. Store in an airtight container in a cool place.

Serves 4

Gajjar Ka Halwa

Carrot Pudding

500 g (1 lb) carrots, peeled and grated
175–250 g (6–8 oz) sugar
900 ml (1½ pints) milk
50 g (2 oz) ghee or butter
25 g (1 oz) sultanas or raisins
8 small green cardamom pods, shelled and seeds ground
15 g (½ oz) almonds, blanched and sliced
15 g (½ oz) sliced or chopped pistachios

Put the grated carrots, sugar and milk in a nonstick or heavy-based pan. Cover and cook gently for 1–1½ hours until the liquid has evaporated.

Add the ghee or butter and sultanas or raisins, increase the heat and fry for about 20 minutes, stirring constantly to prevent the mixture sticking to the bottom of the pan. During this stage the colour will darken.

Remove from the heat and add the ground cardamom seeds. Mix well and pour into a serving dish. Smooth the surface with a wet spatula and sprinkle the nuts evenly on top. Serve hot or cold.

Serves 4

left: *spiced semolina dessert*
above: *gajjar ka halwa*

Shrikhand

Yogurt Pudding

500 g (1 lb) curd cheese
125 g (4 oz) full fat soft cheese
150 g (5 oz) natural yogurt
125–175 g (4–6 oz) icing sugar
10–15 small green cardamom pods, shelled and seeds ground
pinch of powdered saffron
To decorate:
sliced almonds and pistachios
fresh orchids or other flowers

Beat the cheeses and yogurt in a mixing bowl until smooth. Gradually add the sugar and continue beating until light and fluffy. Stir in the ground cardamom seeds and saffron with a metal spoon. Pour into one large dish or four individual serving dishes and decorate with sliced nuts and fresh flowers. Chill before serving.

Serves 4

Banana Halwa

6 large bananas, cut into chunks
3 tablespoons ghee
300 ml (½ pint) water
175 g (6 oz) sugar
½ teaspoon ground cardamom
¼ teaspoon rose essence

Heat the ghee in a pan over a moderate heat and fry the bananas, stirring, for 4–5 minutes until soft. Remove from the heat and mash the bananas until smooth with 3 tablespoons of the water.

Return the pan to the heat and cook for 2–3 minutes, stirring constantly. In a separate pan, dissolve the sugar in the remaining water over a low heat. Pour the syrup over the bananas. Continue cooking, stirring, for 15–20 minutes until the mixture is thick. Stir in the cardamom and rose essence.

Spread the mixture into a 15 x 10 cm (6 x 4 inch) buttered dish. Leave to cool. Cut into squares and chill.

Serves 8

Rawa Halwa

Semolina Pudding

175 g (6 oz) coarse semolina
175 g (6 oz) ghee or unsalted butter
125 g (4 oz) sugar
10–15 small green cardamom pods, shelled and seeds ground
25 g (1 oz) blanched almonds, sliced
25 g (1 oz) sultanas or raisins
450 ml (¾ pint) water or milk
To decorate:
almonds
lime slices

Gently dry roast the semolina in a heavy-based or nonstick pan until light brown. Add the ghee or butter and fry for 5–7 minutes, stirring, until golden brown.

Over a low heat, stir in the sugar, ground cardamom seeds, almonds, and sultanas or raisins. Fry gently for 1 minute, stirring constantly. Stir in the water or milk, cover and leave on a low heat for 1–2 minutes. Stir, then increase the heat and cook for 2–3 minutes until the mixture is thick. Serve hot or cold, decorated with almonds and lime slices.

Serves 4

above left: *shrikhand*
right: *chawal ki kheer*

Chawal Ki Kheer

Rice Pudding

A *kheer*, or *payasam*, is very similar to a milk pudding and it is the most popular sweet dish in India. It can also be made with sago or rice vermicelli and flavoured with rosewater, *kewra* water, saffron, coconut milk or vanilla. Sliced fruits such as banana, mango, apple, orange or dates can also be added when the *kheer* has cooled.

1 teaspoon ghee or butter
1 cm (½ inch) cinnamon stick
125 g (4 oz) coarse semolina or ground rice
1.2 litres (2 pints) milk
175 g (6 oz) sugar
25 g (1 oz) sultanas
10–15 small green cardamom pods, shelled and seeds ground
25 g (1 oz) blanched almonds, sliced or chopped

Melt the ghee or butter in a heavy-based or nonstick pan. Add the cinnamon and fry for 30 seconds. Add the semolina or rice and half of the milk, and stir.

Cover the pan and cook for 15–20 minutes until soft. Mash the mixture, then stir in the sugar and the remaining milk. Simmer gently for 20–25 minutes, stirring constantly to prevent the kheer sticking to the base of the pan. By this time the kheer should be thick. Add the sultanas and check for sweetness. If the kheer is too thick, add a little extra milk or water and cook gently for 5–6 minutes.

Remove from the heat and pour into a serving dish. Stir in the ground cardamom seeds and decorate with nuts. This dish can be served hot or cold and is especially good if chilled in the refrigerator before serving.

Serves 4–6

Variations: When using coarse semolina or ground rice a deliciously mild toffee flavour can be achieved by the following method. Boil the milk until it has reduced by one quarter. Add the rice and sugar and cook for 15 minutes, stirring occasionally. Any grains of rice that slightly stick to the base of the pan will produce a light brown result and the mild toffee flavour. Stir in the ground cardamom and sultanas. Remove from the heat and cover. Decorate with nuts.

To add flavourings such as rosewater or *kewra* water, stir in 3–4 drops when the *kheer* has cooled.

Almond Barfi

Almond Fudge

750 ml (1¼ pints milk)
50 g (2 oz) caster sugar
50 g (2 oz) ground almonds
seeds from 6 small cardamom pods, crushed

Pour the milk into a large heavy-based saucepan and heat gently, uncovered, for about 45 minutes until it is reduced to a thick consistency. Stir occasionally and do not let the milk burn.

When the milk has reduced and thickened, stir in the sugar, then add the ground almonds and cook for 2 minutes. Spread on a buttered shallow dish and sprinkle with the crushed cardamom. Serve warm, cut into wedges or diamond shapes.

Serves 4

Gulab Jaman

Milk Balls in Syrup

375 g (12 oz) sugar
750 ml (1¼ pints) water
4 drops rosewater or kewra water
7 tablespoons low-fat powdered milk
3 teaspoons self-raising flour
1 teaspoon semolina
3 teaspoons ghee
8 small green cardamom pods, shelled and seeds ground
pinch of powdered saffron
milk, to mix
oil, for deep-frying

Put the sugar and water into a large heavy-based or nonstick pan and heat gently to dissolve the sugar. Increase the heat and boil for 2–3 minutes to make a syrup. Stir in the rosewater or kewra water and set the syrup aside.

Put the powdered milk, flour, semolina, ghee, ground cardamom seeds and saffron into a bowl. Mix well with a little milk to make a soft dough. Divide the mixture into 20–22 equal portions, and roll each one into a ball.

Heat the oil and gently deep-fry the milk balls over a low heat until golden brown. Remove with a slotted spoon and transfer to the syrup. When all the milk balls are cooked bring the syrup to boiling point, then remove from the heat. Serve hot or cold.

Serves 4–6

above: *gulab jaman*
right: *baisen barfi*

Baisen Barfi

Chickpea Flour Fudge

Baisen or chickpea flour is popular in Indian cooking and can be brought from Asian food stores. Take care when frying it because although the flour must be thoroughly cooked to avoid any raw flavour, it also burns easily.

375 g (12 oz) ghee or unsalted butter
300 g (10 oz) baisen flour, sifted
300 ml (½ pint) water
375 g (12 oz) sugar
10 small green cardamom pods, shelled and seeds ground
40 g (1¼ oz) mixed unsalted nuts, sliced, e.g. almonds, pistachios and cashew nuts
salt

Grease a 20 x 25 cm (8 x 10 inch) baking dish. Melt the ghee or butter in a nonstick or a heavy-based pan, and gently fry the baisen flour for 5–6 minutes, stirring constantly, until light brown. Remove from the heat.

To make a thick sugar syrup, put the water in a saucepan with the sugar and heat until the sugar dissolves. Bring to the boil and boil for 5 minutes until the syrup is light golden and has thickened. Remove a small spoonful and let it cool slightly; it should form a single strand between the finger and thumb. If the syrup becomes too thick add a little water.

Add the fried baisen flour to the syrup and cook on a low heat for 10–15 minutes, stirring constantly, until the mixture comes away from the sides of the pan and forms a ball. Remove from the heat, stir in a pinch of salt, the ground cardamom seeds and nuts. Pour into the greased dish and smooth the surface with a wet spatula. Leave to cool then cut into cubes or diamond shapes.

Serves 4–6

Pistachio Kulfi

Indian Ice Cream with Pistachios

300 ml (½ pint) double cream
300 ml (½ pint) milk
425 g (14 oz) can condensed milk
1 tablespoon clear honey
2 tablespoons chopped pistachios
2 teaspoons rosewater
green food colouring (optional)

Put the cream, milk, condensed milk and honey into a heavy-based saucepan. Bring gently to the boil, stirring constantly, then simmer for 45 minutes over a very low heat. Remove the pan from the heat, sprinkle in the pistachios and rosewater, then add a little food colouring if liked. Leave to cool.

Pour the mixture into a shallow 900 ml (1½ pint) freezer container or 6–8 kulfi moulds and freeze for 3–4 hours. Remove from the freezer and leave to stand at room temperature for 20–30 minutes to soften.

To serve, turn out the kulfi moulds or cut into squares.

Serves 6–8

Coconut Ice Cream

350 ml (12 fl oz) milk
75 g (3 oz) desiccated coconut
350 ml (12 fl oz) single cream
2 eggs
2 egg yolks
125 g (4 oz) sugar
¼ teaspoon salt

Put the milk, coconut and cream into a heavy-based pan over a low heat and bring just to boiling point. Cook for about 15–20 minutes. Push through a fine sieve, pressing out as much of the coconut juice as possible. Discard the coconut.

Beat the eggs and egg yolks, sugar and salt with an electric beater until thick and mousse-like. Place over a pan of simmering water, stir in some of the coconut cream mixture, then the remainder and cook until the mixture will coat the back of a spoon. Cool quickly, then pour into a freezer container and freeze until mushy. Beat to break up the ice crystals, then return the ice cream to the freezer and freeze for 2–3 hours until firm.

Take the ice cream from the refrigerator about 30 minutes before serving – this helps to soften it so that it is easy to scoop.

Makes about 900 ml (1½ pints)

Carrot Halwa

1.2 litres (2 pints) milk
250 g (8 oz) carrots, finely grated
75 g (3 oz) butter
1 tablespoon golden syrup
125 g (4 oz) sugar
50 g (2 oz) sultanas or raisins
1 teaspoon cardamom seeds, crushed

Place the milk and carrots in a heavy-based pan and cook over a high heat, stirring occasionally, until the liquid has evaporated.

Add the butter, syrup, sugar and sultanas and raisins. Stir until the butter and sugar have melted, then cook for 15–20 minutes, stirring frequently, until the mixture starts to leave the sides of the pan.

Pour into a shallow buttered dish and spread evenly. Sprinkle with the crushed cardamoms. Cut into slices and serve warm or cold.

Serves 4–6

Saffron Lassi

3 tablespoons hot milk
15 saffron threads
½ teaspoon cumin seeds
300 g (10 oz) thick natural yogurt
¼ teaspoon salt
1 teaspoon caster sugar
300 ml (½ pint) water, chilled
cracked ice cubes, to serve

Pour the milk over the saffron and set aside for 1–2 hours to soak.

Heat a frying pan until hot then add the cumin seeds and toast for 1–2 minutes or until you can smell the cumin. Remove from the heat and leave to cool.

Put the yogurt, salt, sugar and water into a food processor and blend for 30 seconds. Add the toasted cumin seeds and blend for 1 minute. Add the soaked saffron liquid to the mixture and blend briefly until combined.

Fill a jug with cracked ice cubes, pour the lassi over the ice and serve.

Serves 4

Lassi

Buttermilk Sherbet

300 g (10 oz) natural yogurt
50 g (2 oz) caster sugar, or to taste
1.2 litres (2 pints) water
salt
To decorate:
ice cubes
shredded lemon rind
mint leaves

Put the yogurt, a pinch of salt and the sugar in a large bowl and beat together thoroughly. Add the water and mix well. Serve in tall glasses decorated with ice, lemon rind and mint leaves.

Serves 4–6

Spiced Tea

5 cm (2 inch) piece of fresh root ginger, peeled and roughly chopped
5 cloves
1 small cinnamon stick
½ teaspoon black peppercorns
3 cardamom pods, bruised
600 ml (1 pint) tea
1–2 tablespoons brown sugar

Place the ginger, cloves, cinnamon, peppercorns, cardamom pods and tea in a saucepan and bring to the boil. Cover the pan and simmer for 10 minutes.

Remove the pan from the heat and strain the tea into another saucepan. Return to the heat with the sugar and heat gently until the sugar has dissolved. Serve black.

***above:** lassi*

Thandai

Milk and Saffron Sherbet

Also known as *kesher doodh*, this is a very popular Indian refreshment and can be made with hot milk too. In many parts of India a little alcohol is added, and the sherbet is drunk during festivals such as Holi (festival of spring) or Diwali (festival of lights). The ground mixture may be prepared in a larger quantity and stored in a sealed jar for several months. This flavouring can also be included in puddings and sweets.

15 g (½ oz) blanched almonds
15 g (½ oz) chopped pistachios
seeds from 10–12 small green cardamom pods
pinch of saffron threads
50 g (2 oz) caster sugar, or to taste
1.2 litres (2 pints) milk, chilled
¼ teaspoon ground turmeric
¼ teaspoon ground nutmeg
crushed ice (optional), to serve

Finely grind the almonds, pistachios, cardamom seeds and saffron threads. Put the sugar in the milk and stir thoroughly until dissolved. Add the turmeric, nutmeg and the ground nuts. Stir well and serve in tall glasses, adding crushed ice if you like.

Serves 4

Aam Ka Sherbet

Mango Sherbet

3 ripe mangoes, halved
1.2 litres (2 pints) water
juice of 1 lemon (optional)
25–50 g (1–2 oz) caster sugar, or to taste
salt
crushed ice, to serve

Squeeze the mango pulp into a bowl and discard the skin and stones. Add the water and stir to mix thoroughly. Add a pinch of salt, the lemon juice and sugar and stir well until dissolved. Serve chilled with crushed ice.

Serves 4–6

Variation: If available unripe green mangoes can also be used. These should be placed under a preheated grill until the pulp feels soft. The skin will split and cracks will appear. Leave the mangoes to cool, then peel off the skin.

Nimbo Pani

Lemon or Lime Sherbet

75 ml (3 fl oz) fresh lemon or lime juice
1 litre (1¾ pints) water
50 g (2 oz) caster sugar, or to taste
8–10 mint leaves or rose petals, washed
salt
ice, to serve
lemon or lime slices, to decorate

Mix the lemon or lime juice with the water in a large jug. Stir in the sugar and a pinch of salt until dissolved. Gently crush the mint leaves or rose petals by hand to release the aromas and add to the sherbet. Serve with ice and twists of lemon or lime.

Serves 4

***right:** clockwise from top left, thandai, phalon ka sherbet (see page 92), masala angoor sherbet (see page 92), aam ka sherbet, nimbo pani*

Masala Angoor Sherbet

Spiced Grape Sherbet

175 g (6 oz) seedless green grapes, plus extra to decorate
1 litre (1¾ pints) water
1 tablespoon lemon juice
about 50 g (2 oz) caster sugar
salt and pepper
ice cubes, to serve

Put the grapes in a blender or food processor and liquidize. Add the water and strain into a jug. Add the lemon juice and stir in the sugar and a pinch of salt until dissolved. Sprinkle with pepper to taste, decorate with the extra grapes and serve with ice.

Serves 4–6

Phalon Ka Sherbet

Mixed Fruit Sherbet

about 125 g (4 oz) caster sugar
300 ml (½ pint) water
juice of 2 lemons
1.2 litres (2 pints) lemonade
1 banana, sliced
1 orange, sliced and quartered
1 apple, quartered and thinly sliced
1 pear, quartered and thinly sliced
2 rings fresh or canned pineapple, thinly sliced
8–10 firm strawberries, hulled and sliced
a few seedless grapes, halved
mint leaves, chopped or crushed by hand
grated rind of 1 lemon
75 ml (3 fl oz) gin or vodka (optional)
crushed ice (optional)

Put the sugar and water into a large jug and stir well until the sugar has dissolved. Stir in the lemon juice and lemonade. Add the fruit and stir gently. Add the mint, lemon rind and gin or vodka, if using. Mix well and serve chilled or with crushed ice.

Serves 8–10

Pistachio Barfi

1 litre (1¾ pints) milk
50 g (2 oz) sugar
75 g (3 oz) chopped pistachios
25 g (1 oz) ground almonds
½ teaspoon cardamom seeds, crushed
few drops of green colouring
edible silver paper (varak), to decorate (optional)

Pour the milk into a heavy pan, bring to the boil and simmer, uncovered, until it has reduced by half. Add the sugar and stir over a low heat to dissolve.

Mix the pistachio nuts, almonds and cardamom seeds and add to the pan. Stir well and continue to cook, stirring, until the mixture is thick. Blend in a few drops of green colouring to give a delicate green colour.

Pour the mixture into a greased shallow dish or tin and decorate with edible silver paper, if liked. Leave to cool, then cut the barfi into squares.

Serves 4

Indian Fruit Salad

25 g (1 oz) block tamarind
1 teaspoon chilli powder
sugar
2 green chillies, thinly sliced (optional)
2.5 cm (1 inch) piece of fresh root ginger, peeled and cut into fine strips
1 each pear, apple and banana or guava, mango and any other fruit, cut into small pieces.

Break up the tamarind and soak in 175 ml (6 fl oz) boiling water for 10–15 minutes then press through a sieve to extract as much liquid as possible. Discard the pulp.

***above right:** phalon ka chat*

Put the tamarind liquid into a bowl, add the chilli powder and sugar to taste and simmer gently for 15–20 minutes. Pour into a bowl, cover and leave to cool.

Stir in the chillies, if using.

Put the fruit into a large serving bowl and add the sauce. Cover and chill until ready to serve.

Serves 4

Phalon Ka Chat

Fruit Savoury

- 2 dessert apples, cored and sliced
- 2–3 bananas, sliced
- 1 pear, peeled and sliced
- 1 orange, segmented and cut in half
- 425 g (14 oz) can sliced peaches, drained
- a few grapes
- ½ cucumber
- 425 g (14 oz) can pineapple chunks, drained
- 425 g (14 oz) can guavas, drained and lightly mashed
- about ½ teaspoon chilli powder
- 1–2 teaspoons black pepper
- 1 small ripe papaya, peeled, deseeded and cubed
- lemon juice, to taste
- salt

In a large bowl mix together the apples, bananas, pear, orange, peaches, grapes, cucumber, pineapple and guavas. Sprinkle with the chilli powder, pepper and a pinch of salt. Add the cubed papaya and sprinkle with lemon juice. Toss all the fruits thoroughly. This fruit salad is a good accompaniment to samosas or kebabs.

Serves 4–6

Walnut Sweet

125 g (4 oz) shelled walnuts
3 tablespoons oil
75 g (3 oz) dates, stoned
900 ml (1½ pints) water
150 g (5 oz) sugar
40 g (1½ oz) ground rice
3 tablespoons milk
apple flower, to decorate (optional)

Soak the walnuts in boiling water for 10 minutes. Drain and remove the skins then dry on kitchen paper.

Heat the oil in a wok or deep frying pan, add the walnuts and fry quickly until lightly browned (take care not to burn them). Drain on kitchen paper.

Grind the walnuts and dates in a blender or food processor. Bring the water to a boil and stir in the nut mixture and sugar. Blend the ground rice with the milk and add to the nut mixture. Bring back to the boil, stirring, and cook for 2 minutes, until thickened.

Spoon into a warmed serving dish, decorate with an apple flower, if liked, and serve hot.

Serves 4–6

Coconut Pudding

For a simple way to open a coconut, put it in a roasting tin and place in a preheated oven, 150°C (300°F), Gas Mark 2, for about 25 minutes. The coconut should crack itself while cooking. Leave to cool then grate the flesh as required.

2 fresh coconuts
450 ml (¾ pint) boiling water
250 g (8 oz) caster sugar
175 g (6 oz) rice flour
2 eggs, beaten
50 g (2 oz) slivered almonds

Prepare the coconuts (see recipe introduction). Grate the coconut flesh into a bowl, then pour on the boiling water. Allow to stand for 15 minutes, then strain the liquid through a sieve lined with a double thickness of muslin held over a bowl. Gather up the muslin and squeeze out as much of the coconut milk as possible. Discard the coconut from inside the cloth. Mix the strained coconut milk with the liquid extracted from the whole coconuts, then beat in the sugar, rice flour, eggs and almonds.

Place the mixture in a large saucepan and bring to the boil. Lower the heat and simmer until the mixture thickens, stirring constantly. Pour into a greased 20 cm (8 inch) round baking tin and bake for about 30 minutes until the top is browned. Serve hot.

Serves 4

above: *walnut sweet*

Coconut Squares

1.2 litres (2 pints) milk
125 g (4 oz) sugar
125 g (4 oz) fresh grated coconut or desiccated coconut
1 teaspoon rosewater
few drops pink colouring
edible silver paper (varak), to decorate (optional)

Pour the milk into a heavy pan, bring to the boil and let it simmer uncovered, until reduced by half, stirring frequently. Add the sugar and stir over a low heat to dissolve. Then stir in the coconut and continue cooking and stirring until the mixture is very thick. Stir in the rosewater.

Turn half the mixture into a greased shallow dish or tin. Add the colouring to the remaining mixture, tinting it a pale pink colour. Then spread on top of the white layer in the tin.

Leave to cool then cut into squares. Decorate with edible silver paper, if liked.

Serves 4

Nan Khatai

Coconut Biscuits

250 g (8 oz) plain flour
1½ teaspoons baking powder
½ teaspoon ground cardamom
½ teaspoon salt
300 g (10 oz) caster sugar
250 g (8 oz) butter, softened
2 eggs, beaten
granulated sugar
desiccated coconut

Sift the flour, baking powder, cardamom and salt. Beat together the caster sugar and butter in a large bowl until the mixture is pale and fluffy. Gradually beat in the eggs, adding a little flour between each addition. Then fold in the remaining flour.

Drop teaspoonfuls of the dough on to ungreased baking sheets, spacing them well apart. Flatten to form small rounds about 3 mm (⅛ inch) thick, using a glass covered with a damp cloth. Sprinkle with granulated sugar and coconut.

Bake in a preheated oven, 190°C (375°F), Gas Mark 5, for 8–10 minutes, or until the biscuits are lightly browned around the edges. Leave them on the baking sheets for about 30 seconds, then transfer to a wire rack and leave to cool. Store in airtight containers until required.

Makes about 60

Vermicelli Pudding

125 g (4 oz) ghee
125 g (4 oz) vermicelli
750 ml (1¼ pints) milk
15 cardamom pods, shelled and seeds ground
250 g (8 oz) clear honey
125 g (4 oz) sultanas

Heat the ghee in a heavy-based pan and add the vermicelli, breaking it into 4 cm (1½ inch) pieces. Fry gently for 5–6 minutes, then pour on the milk and bring to the boil.

Sprinkle the ground cardamom seeds into the pan and add the honey, spoonful by spoonful. Stir well until the honey has melted. Cook for a further 10–15 minutes, then stir in the sultanas. Serve hot or chilled.

Serves 6

Index